Women in Business in Early Modern Copenhagen

Women in Business in Early Modern Copenhagen

1740–1835

Carol Gold

MUSEUM TUSCULANUM PRESS

Women in Business in Early Modern Copenhagen, 1740–1835
Carol Gold

Copy editor: Jordy Findanis
Layout, composition, and cover design: Erling Lynder
Printed in Denmark by Tarm Bogtryk
ISBN 978 87 635 4597 6

Cover illustration: Peter Cramer, *Street Seller,*
1780, 23 × 19 cm, oil on canvas,
Copenhagen City Museum.

An earlier version of Chapter Two, "On the Streets and in the Markets: Independent Copenhagen Saleswomen," appeared in *Gender in the European Town: Female Agency in the Urban Economy, 1640–1830*, ed. Deborah Simonton and Anne Montenach (London: Routledge, 2013), pp. 35–55. I would like to thank the publisher for kind permission to reprint the article in this volume.

The book is published with financial support from
E. Lerager Larsens Fond

Museum Tusculanum Press
Dantes Plads 1
1556 Copenhagen S
Denmark
www.mtp.dk

Table of Contents

Acknowledgments

Writing up acknowledgments allows me to take time to remember all the people who have helped me over the past ten years. It serves as a fond walk down memory lane. It started with the unexpected pleasure and delight of discovering that there were indeed other historians interested in the same issues about which I was writing. In the summer of 2008, I attended a conference "Nordic Women Historians" in Reykjavik, Iceland, and participated in a series of sessions organized by a working group on "Gender in the European Town." As a European historian working on Danish women's history in Fairbanks, Alaska, I was often very lonely in my research. Here, in Reykjavik, I found an entire group of historians dedicated to the research of similar issues. I cannot overstate the importance this group played in my work. Over the years and several conferences later, they read my work, commented on my work, gave me ideas and inspiration, and encouraged my efforts for a decade. The group was organized and supported by Deborah Simonton, then of the University of Southern Denmark, now retired. Debbi not only brought us all together, she organized and found funding for the group, encouraged and supported our work, and eventually found publications opportunities. Over the years Debbi has also become a good friend. So, to Debbi, a heartfelt "thank you." This would have been a much poorer work without your help and support.

Through "Gender and the European Town" I also learned to know Anne Montenach, of the University of Aix-Marseille. Anne read several of my articles as well as the manuscript of this book in draft stage. For her help, support and suggestions I am also extremely grateful.

Invaluable help with research came from the staff at the Copenhagen City Archives. They were always ready with suggestions, ideas, and assistance in reading the old Danish Gothic writing. Nete Wingender, now retired, was of inestimable help accessing archival material and remains a friend today. But I specifically want to mention Lars Peter Jørgensen, now deceased, for his unstinting help and suggestions. Lars Peter would suddenly show up with material which "might be of interest," and always was. He was also a past master at reading the Gothic handwriting. Søren Bitsch Christensen, now Århus city archivist, was instrumental in locating material from the Danish Merchants Society (*Grosserer-Societetet*).

Two historian-curators—Jørgen Larsen of *Berlingske Tidende* and Adam Grandjean of *Danske Bank*—were friendly and helpful in showing me around their old buildings and discussing the eighteenth-century inhabitants with me. It's hard to overstate how encouraging it is to find others who "know" the people one is writing about. I must also take a moment to rave about how well cared for both "*de gamle stuer*" ("the old rooms") in the Berlingske House and the first/second floor of Erichsen's Mansion (Danske Bank's building) are. They give a sense of walking back in time, into eighteenth-century interiors.

Genealogists and academic historians often approach history from very different angles. And yet, just that difference opens up possible avenues of research that I, for one, had not previously considered. So many thanks go to Peter Edelberg and Joao Guimaraes, both of whom contacted me with information and material about their families. Peter is a descendant of Else Fenger; he provided family stories and pictures. Else owned and managed a soap factory on Christianshavn for over twenty years. Joao, a Brazilian, who now lives in New York City, found an article I wrote online while researching his family. He is a descendant of Peter Erichsen. Peter was Erich Erichsen's brother, and Erich was Johanne Wadum's second husband. Johanne owned an import-export firm in the late eighteenth century. Both men's enthusiasm for their ancestors inspired me to dig a little deeper to find more information about the people in their families.

Sheri Layral, Myra LeWinter, Mary Mangusso, Ole Hyldtoft, Maria Hilden, and Bernhard Brackhahn, long-time friends, all read drafts in various stages, encouraged, supported, and were infinitely patient in talking with me about this decade-long project.

Finally, Susan Wladaver-Morgan, long-time friend and sister historian, copy-edited the manuscript (I fiddled, so all remaining mistakes are still mine) and created the index.

Many, many thanks to all of you for your on-going help, support and patience.

List of Tables, Charts, and Figures

Appendices

Chapter One

Introduction

It is an unacknowledged truth that women have always worked. Single, married, widowed, they have worked inside and outside the home. Sometimes they received pay for this work; sometimes it was as an unpaid part of a "family economy." Often women's work in the household went unrecognized as part of the ideology of "domesticity." Seen or unseen, rewarded or not, families, households, and the economy could not have functioned without women's contributions. Their occupations ran the gamut of the possible. Wherever men have worked, women could and often did as well, with a very few notable exceptions such as government, the military, and the clergy. Women had places everywhere else. They were so ubiquitous that they did not stand out, were not noticed, and hence often invisible.

Anette Lucie Benedicte Linde (1763–1815) owned and ran a private, proprietary school for girls from the time of her marriage until her death twenty-eight years later. Madame Linde's school was one of the largest in Copenhagen, enrolling as many as a hundred girls, both day and boarding students. Her husband, Georg Christopher Lorentz Linde, was a master goldsmith, head of the goldsmith's guild, and a member of Copenhagen's ruling City Council, "The 32 Men." Both Anette and Georg lived and worked at the same address, Raadhusstræde 8, but the two businesses had nothing to do with each other. Both spouses managed their own businesses, with separate licenses, permissions, and guild affiliations. The Lindes' story challenges the standard women's history narrative that early modern women worked only with husbands in an urban "family economy."[1]

In 1801, Bodil Kirstine Johansen paid taxes as a blacksmith. Although a widow, she was allowed to continue in her husband's profession on her own. Karen Mariager received permission in 1793 not only to continue in her husband's trade as a ropemaker after his death, but also to employ and train apprentices, suggesting the assumption that this would be a multi-year occupation. Madame Storch, of Lille Torvegade in Copenhagen, paid taxes in 1771 as a glazier. She may have been a widow; the records do not say. What these women have in common is that they all worked in industries not usually associated with women's work. As widows, they were allowed to continue in their husbands' occupations. Beyond these examples women were to be found throughout the early modern urban economy, in unexpected as well as predictable places. Making up perhaps 10 percent of the urban work force, neither the city nor their families could have functioned without them.

This book explores the lives and stories of women in eighteenth- and early nineteenth-century preindustrial Copenhagen who worked on their own. In order to be considered "on her own," a woman had to have had some official contact with a government or guild body. Thus, the book focuses on women who behaved legally, who applied for and received the necessary licenses and permits, and who paid taxes. These women were to be found throughout the entire urban economy. They were married, widowed, and single. As with the Lindes, married women often worked "on their own." They did not automatically participate in a family economy; sometimes they did, but often they did not. Schoolteaching and goldsmithing are not related occupations, yet both Anette and Georg carried on their separate businesses within the space of the same household and building.

This book deals only with women in the visible, legal economy; it does not include women in the grey or black markets. It also deals only with jobs that required official permission, thus excluding boarding house keepers and laundresses. Since it deals only with legal occupations, women who worked as prostitutes are also excluded, nor does it consider women who were salaried by others. This is not a study of *all* working women. Rather, it is a study of those women who were legal and independent, whose work was registered in their own names. In other words, it is a study of the extent of the *possible,* of legal options that were available to women. It was possible for married women to carry on their own businesses, possible for a woman to work as a glazier or a ropemaker. The fact that some women were engaged in these professions meant that other women could also view these as viable options.

These boundaries were drawn partly because this is a group who left records, but also because this group is often overlooked. As Laurel Thatcher Ulrich noted, "well-behaved women seldom make history."[2] She did not mean that such women are not to be found on the barricades, but rather that they are seldom to be found in the archives. When she wrote that, much women's history had focused on women who had misbehaved; court records offered a fruitful source for historians, and unruly women were obviously visible. Finding well-behaved women is much more difficult, particularly in large cities where there are simply so many people.

The standard women's history narrative is that, while early modern urban women did indeed work, they worked together with husbands in a "family economy." That is, if the husband was a shoemaker, he cobbled the shoes (the skilled part of the job), while his wife and perhaps children stitched the uppers and worked in the shop. Thus, the entire family presumably participated in the work together, under the auspices of the husband, who may have been the family "breadwinner," but who certainly could not have done the entire job on his own. Many married women often disappeared into husbands' official and archival records. "Seldom," however, is not always, and this research has shown that it is possible to find "well-behaved" women who worked on their own.

Literature on Women's Work

Generations of women's historians have been attempting to explain and nuance the reality of working women. In 1919, Alice Clark wrote about a "golden age" for working women in seventeenth-century England, an economic system of "Family Industry," in which husbands, wives, and children all worked together and profits "belonged to the family." In the seventeenth century, "the idea is seldom encountered that a man supports his wife; husband and wife were then mutually dependent." This idyll, Clark argued, was destroyed by the inroads of capitalism and the development of "Industrialism," a period in which men's work moved outside of the home while women remained within the home, now solely responsible for "domestic work, *viz,* cooking, cleaning, mending, tending of children, etc."[3]

Against the background of the second wave women's movement in the mid-twentieth century and women's push for meaningful employment outside the home, historians Joan Scott and Louise Tilly argued that women had always worked as an integral part of a family unit. There was nothing new in the concept of a working women or working wife. "[T]he household or the family is the crucial economic unit. ... It is simply assumed that women will work, for their contribution is valued as necessary for the survival of the family unit." They referred to this as "family economy,"[4] a label and concept that they reemphasized in their 1978 book, *Women, Work, and Family,*[5] and that has continued in the literature.

In 1986-87, the Danish National Museum in Copenhagen mounted an exhibit on "Women's Business and Handwork in the Eighteenth Century." In conjunction with the exhibit, the curators put together an exhibition catalog which was then followed up with an article in *Siden Saxo* (Since Saxo), a journal of popular history in Denmark. Both the exhibit and the article detailed the various economic activities in which eighteenth-century Danish women (mostly urban) engaged. The authors concluded "that as a married woman she supplemented her family's income—either directly by working in her husband's artisanal production—or with her own business, as for instance laundress, spinster, midwife, schoolkeeper or saleswoman." Of middle-class wives, they wrote that they also often worked outside the home, making enough to support themselves and sometimes their families as well. "The 200 years between the eighteenth century and our times is the only period in modern history during which middle-class women were bound to the home as mothers and housewives."[6] Tantalizing as their conclusions are, there was no follow-up. They did not investigate the matter further, nor describe it more fully.

These authors were writing against the then-standard narrative of "separate spheres," which placed women in the home with domestic and reproductive responsibilities. They showed how women have always had productive responsibilities as well. While it is undoubtedly true that a large number of women who worked in preindustrial urban economies did so within the context of a family economy—that is, worked with and alongside of husbands who officially represented and supported the family—there was also a sizable number of women whose work took them outside their husbands' businesses and whose contribution to the family's economy took place in fields or businesses different and separate from those of their husbands. Their earnings still contributed to the family, but more in the pattern of the two-income families with which we are familiar today. It is time to further nuance the standard narrative.

Recent literature on the subject is beginning to deal with independent working women. Hannah Barker argued, in her 2006 study of businesswomen in northern England, that they "were central to urban society and to the operation and development of commerce in the late eighteenth and early nineteenth centuries." Women did not remain in the home, but moved to larger urban centers in order to find gainful employment.[7] Nicola Phillips reported similar findings in her work from the same year, noting that "this book provides evidence of women in business operating as fully integrated members of local trading networks, exchanging money, credit, property and goods with males traders on a regular basis throughout the period."[8]

Recently, "Gender in the European Town," a working network, has published a series of books addressing aspects of gendered experience in early modern urban settings. *Female Agency in the Urban Economy*, edited by Deborah Simonton and Anne Montenach, contains several essays on the subject, further nuancing the narrative of a family economy and highlighting women working in an urban economic setting.[9]

Married women working separately from their husbands was not a new idea for me. I had written a book on private schools for girls in late eighteenth-century Copenhagen; these were for-profit schools owned and run by women. One-third of these schoolkeepers were married at the time they received permission for their schools.[10] While it was certainly true that there was a group of married women whose husbands also had schools, sometimes in the same apartment and sharing the same teachers, many wives had school licenses in their own names, separate from their husbands' business licenses. In fact, 83 percent of these women's husbands worked in fields far removed from education, similar to the Lindes' experience.[11]

There were also midwives who by legal definition had to be married and whose husbands obviously did not work alongside them. Were these examples just anomalies, or did they represent the possibility of other married women working in their own names? My research shows that about three-quarters of the independent working women whose marital status we know were married at the time they received a license or paid tax on self-employment income in their own names. That is, there were large numbers of women who were married at the moment of their contact with government or guild authorities, and they were doing business separate from their husbands. If it had been a husband's business, the wife's name would not have appeared in legal records. So if we know the wife's name, we also know she was at that moment working independently of her husband.

At the specific moment of their involvement with government or guild authorities, 73 percent of legally employed women were married; 24 percent were widowed, and the remaining 3 percent single. None of these women were working with husbands in a "family economy." They were working on their own, in their own names. Even if there were a husband in the picture somewhere, he was not in her business.

Chart 1.1

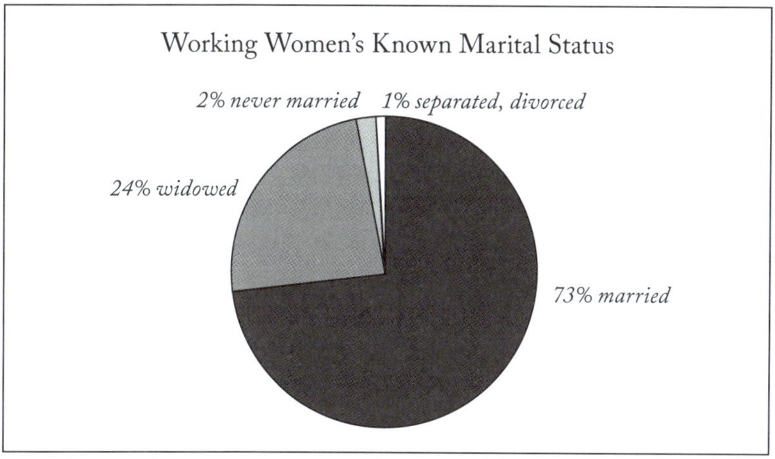

General Background

Until 1849 Denmark was an absolute monarchy that accorded complete and total power to its hereditary male monarch. In 1784 the young crown prince, Frederik (later to be Frederik VI), took over personal control of the government in a palace coup against his father, King Christian VII, who was certifiably insane. This moment marked the beginning of a new "reform era," filled with liberal reforms that succeeded in changing the landscape, the society, and the economy of the country. The two best-known of these reforms was the abolition of *stavnsbaandet*, a law that tied most male peasants to their place of birth, and the redistribution of land (at a price) to the peasants who worked it.[12] These newly freed, "self-owning" (i.e., owning their own land) peasants were to form the backbone of the Danish economy as independent farmers through the mid-twentieth century. Other reforms involved the elimination of most tariffs and the introduction of free trade, the end of the slave trade, the introduction of compulsory education (for girls as well as boys), citizenship for Jews, revisions of poor help, the penal code, and the prison system. In short, the late eighteenth century was a period of dramatic change in Danish society.

Economically, the country flourished under the new regime. Danish neutrality and the merchant marine helped to supply the country during the early years of the French and Napoleonic Wars. However, in 1807 the British attacked Copenhagen, bombing the city with incendiary bombs that set parts of the downtown ablaze and destroyed much of the city. The British then sailed off with the Danish fleet, ending Danish neutrality for the rest of the Napoleonic period. In fact, by 1814 Denmark was Napoleon's last and only ally. Under the terms of the Treaty of Kiel, Denmark lost Norway to Sweden in 1814. The war had taxed the Danish treasury so badly that the government declared bankruptcy in 1813, even before its end. The resulting economic depression continued through the 1830s.

At the center of this activity was the royal residence city—Copenhagen. Its Danish name, *København*, literally translates as "buying harbor," or "merchants harbor."

> It is the capital and royal residence, the site of the country's most important trade, the main fortress of the realm; here is the only university for the dual kingdoms [Denmark and Norway]; the navy and the royal arsenal are here; all the important manufacturers and factories are concentrated here; and the art academy and theater are here;—in a word, everything interesting and remarkable which Denmark has to display is to be found in Copenhagen.[13]

The Copenhagen that Rasmus Nyerup described in 1800, before the fire and bankruptcy, was indeed a thriving city. With a population of just over 100,000, it housed the royal residence, a large army base, and a major naval port. Military personnel accounted for approximately 20 percent of the total population, which meant there were slightly more men in the city than women (a ratio of fifty-one men to forty-nine women).[14] It had an active harbor with shipping and merchant facilities. Danish history refers to this period as the "palmy days," and, indeed, much money was made and passed through the city, and extravagant new houses were built in bouts of conspicuous consumption. This is also the "Golden Age" of Danish art and literature. But the city contained much more—all those people at the other end of the social structure who provided the services and made such "golden" living possible. From the soldiers and sailors, who were supposed to defend the realm yet ultimately failed to do so, through the salespeople and producers, who supplied the city with home-grown and imported goods, up to the merchants, who ran international shipping companies, Copenhagen was a vibrant, exciting, flourishing urban center.

Along with shipping, Copenhagen's main industry was service. The city serviced the royal residence and bureaucracy, the army and naval bases, and the large merchant marine. Civil servants and military personnel together accounted for about 30 percent of the city's population. What this means is not that Copenhageners did not produce anything, but that most of what was produced in the city was for city use. With the exception of overseas goods, which were brought into the city and then sold elsewhere in the country as well as further north, most of Copenhagen's products remained in the city, bought by city residents for their own use. For example, the industry with the single largest number of individual taxpayers in 1801 was the retail beer-dispensing business; 504 men and 34 women paid taxes as beer dispensers (*øltappere*) in 1801. This was almost twice as many individuals as the next two largest groups, shoemakers and small shopkeepers (*høkere*), with 296 and 279 taxpayers (men and women) respectively. There were also 239 distillers of hard liquor (*brændevinsbrændere*).[15] Fewer shipping merchants may have paid much more in taxes, but, in terms of sheer numbers of people involved in any given industry, those who serviced a local clientele made up the majority.

In terms of value, though, shipping was the largest industry in Copenhagen. Historian Svend Aage Hansen refers to the overseas trade and shipping industries as "the period's most obvious growth-promoting factor."[16] In 1800, there were 327 merchant ships operating out of Copenhagen, with a total carrying capacity of 25,792 *kommercelæster*.[17] The Danish merchant marine was the fourth largest in Europe, and Ole Feldbæk estimates that "Copenhagen, during its palmy period, was actually the city in Europe that had the largest per capita shipping and trade."[18] The merchants who owned these ships, either singly or in joint stock companies, were among the wealthiest people in Copenhagen, and the fancy new houses they built literally changed the face of the city.

Danish shipping interests spanned the world. The record book for the Danish Merchant Association from 1774 to 1790 lists Danish consuls in Cartagena, Bayonne, Riga, Livorno, Cadiz, the Mediterranean, Bilbao, Cagliari (Sardinia), the north coast of Spain, Normandy, Nantes, Liverpool, Memel, Great Britain, Gothenburg, Tangier, Nice, St. Petersburg, and Malaga. In addition, the records discuss trade with the West Indies, the Levant, Flensburg, Portugal, Kiel, the East Indies, France, and Spain.[19]

The eighteenth century was the highpoint of the Danish "empire." In addition to Norway, Greenland, Iceland, and the Faroe Islands, Denmark also owned three islands in the West Indies (St. Thomas, St. Croix, and St. John—today's U.S. Virgin Islands) and some forts along the west coast of Africa and on the Indian subcontinent. Though it was not a large empire by that time's imperial standards and, except for the West Indian islands, it was mostly just stopping-off and refueling spots, the West Indies did provide another major ingredient for Danish industry—sugar. The Danish West Indian-Guianese Company established a sugar refinery in Copenhagen as early as 1720,[20] and by 1770, fifteen refineries were operating in Copenhagen. In 1788, Copenhagen sugar refineries processed 16.5 million pounds of sugar. Sugar—raw, refined, and as syrup—accounted for two-thirds of Copenhagen's exports at the time.[21]

With sugar, of course, came slavery. Although there were no slaves in Denmark proper, much money flowed into Copenhagen through the slave trade and the transport and sale of products made possible by slavery on the Danish West Indian islands. It should be noted that Denmark was the first country to start to outlaw the slave trade. The ordinance outlawing trade in humans was issued in 1792, but it allowed a ten-year grace period in order to enable slaveowners to stock up on this valuable commodity. As the 1803 cutoff point approached, slave owners in the Danish West Indies petitioned for additional time. The Danish commission was still "studying" the matter in 1807, when the English passed a law outlawing the slave trade, thus preempting the Danes.[22] Slavery itself was not outlawed in the Danish West Indies until 1848.

Although they produced somewhat less in absolute wealth, budding new industries and older manufactories also thrived in the city. The Royal Copenhagen Porcelain Factory, still in existence today, was founded in 1775, with royal support. There had been an earlier porcelain and stoneware factory, started in 1723, but what became of it is unknown. However, textiles were probably the most important factory production. As early as 1730, there were three wool manufactories operating in the city. These were followed quickly by stocking, linen, and ribbon mills.[23] Indeed, according to Ole Feldbæk, "production [in Copenhagen] was predominantly textile production." Silk weaving, which had reached a peak in the 1760s with 303 looms, was on its way out by the end of the century. It was being replaced by factories that dyed imported Indian cotton fabric, of which there were sixteen in 1798, employing 598 people.[24] Note that silk and cotton mills would necessarily be dependent on an overseas trade in raw materials, whereas earlier textile mills probably depended on materials available closer to home, such as wool and flax.

Copenhagen, circa 1800, was the administrative capital of the Danish realm, an important international shipping port, and the royal residence. As such, it was in an anomalous position. Technically, Copenhagen had its own government, with a city council ("The 32 Men") chosen by the Magistrates from among names put forward by The 32 Men. These city fathers were chosen for life, and all came from the same upper-middle-class circles; generally they were related to each other as well. The Magistrates, for their part, were all chosen by the king, generally from the nobility, and felt themselves to be representatives of royal authority. There was a shifting number of Magistrates, generally three or four mayors, or section heads, and six to eight councilmen. Considerable tension existed between the two groups—The 32 Men on the one hand and the Magistrates on the other. Who controlled the administration of the city? Perhaps more importantly, who controlled administration of the city's economy? According to Flemming Dahl, The 32 Men were able to retain control over "business life" and "the city's economic and financial conditions." He concludes, "the business life of the capital city was the special province of The 32 Men, which they watched over with care and protected with zeal."[25]

Copenhagen's geography in the late eighteenth century was still that of a medieval city. Despite the fact that much of the city had burned down twice during the 1700s, in October 1728 and June 1795, it was rebuilt along basically the same pattern of narrow, winding medieval lanes. There were plans to broaden streets, but the government bureaucracy took so long that people simply rebuilt where their houses had stood. Much of inner-city Copenhagen today dates back to the rebuilding after the 1795 fire. The city was surrounded by walls, with gates that were closed at night. Anyone not a legal resident of the city was supposed to be outside the city walls by nightfall. Many of the entries in the police blotter deal with illegal "vagrants" and prostitutes—people without fixed abodes or occupations in the city.[26] In 1801, an exception was made allowing people with medical emergencies, including imminent childbirth, to enter through Nørreport, the northern gate.[27]

Copenhagen was a densely populated city. Richard Willerslev estimates that in 1801, there were 980 apartments in the city, and, although the average space per person was relatively generous (15.7 square meters or 141 square feet per person); most people had much less room. Twelve percent of the city's residents lived in apartments with just five square meters (forty-five square feet) per person. Fifty-six percent of residents lived in apartments with one or two rooms, which might or might not include a kitchen.[28] An advertisement in *Adresseavisen* from August 30, 1791, for example, offered the following, "On the corner of Compagnie- and Raadhuusstræde no. 44, where the street door is kept locked, one floor consisting of 4 rooms ensuite, with cellar, wash cellar, etc. for a small family to rent."[29] No kitchen is mentioned. And although the average number of inhabitants per apartment was 4.5, nonetheless, over half (56 percent) of Copenhageners lived in apartments housing only two to four people, implying that families and households were relatively small.[30]

Of course, these are averages, and life on Christianshavn and in Skt. Annæ Vest was much more crowded than life in the elegant Strand quarter or around Kongens Nytorv (the King's New Square). But all shared the same streets and marketplaces, and, according to K.H. Seidelin, editor and writer of *Politivennen* (The Police Friend), a weekly "scandal sheet," the city lacked many modern amenities. He complained of gutters overflowing into the streets, unshoveled streets, potholes, broken tiles, loud drunks, dogs, and pimps and madams who preyed on young women and inexperienced youths. He wanted to have street signs painted on corner buildings, peoples' names put on street doors, and for public parks and walks to have more benches.[31]

Walking through downtown Copenhagen today, one can get a sense of the landscape of the city, of the narrow streets, low buildings, and open spaces of markets and church yards. But we lack the noise and the smell and the sense of living in such close proximity with so many other people doing so many things in the common public spaces. Quaint and clean as the city may seem to us today, we have no way of understanding how people at the time viewed it, yet Seidelin's complaints may open a small window on the idea that even in the nineteenth century people did not readily accept the noise and pollution.

Women's Legal Status

Women in early modern Denmark could not be "citizens" of towns or cities and never received *borgerbreve* (citizenship letters that gave permission to carry on a specified business or occupation).[32] Married women were technically *femmes couvertes*, subject to their husbands and dependent on husbands' permissions in order to act in any independent civil matter. Yet women were acting on their own and had long been doing so, certainly since the Middle Ages. Legally, Danish married women had no independence under coverture until the law was changed in 1880, but the reality was much different. The default regarding women's legal status apparently changed sometime during the early modern period. Going back to the Middle Ages, a married woman had to have her husband's express permission to enter into a contract or to conduct independent business. However, by the eighteenth century the reality had changed so that a married woman acting on her own was assumed to have her husband's permission. Unless he actively disapproved or stopped her in some way, the assumption was that she had his authorization.[33] This was, of course, a huge loophole, which would allow women to function as de facto *femme sole*, rather than the official *femme couverte*.

The other official constraints on women's work were guilds and guild regulations. Guilds controlled a sizable part of the Danish urban economy in the late eighteenth century. This continued despite the fact that the Danish absolutist state was on the offensive against guilds and allowed the establishment of more and more businesses outside of the formal guild structure, including the existence of a growing number of "free" craftsmen, who had permission to work outside of the guilds.[34] Women were not allowed to join guilds, but they could and did receive permits or licenses (*næringsbreve*) to work in guild trades, often as widows or as divorcées.

Economically, there was no functional difference between a *borgerbrev* (citizenship) and a *næringsbrev* (business permit), but politically there was. "Citizens" could vote in the guilds, vote in municipal elections for members of the city council (The 32 Men), and were responsible for helping in the upkeep and defense of the city. "Citizens" had a certain authority in the towns. Women could do none of these things, nor did they have the status that went with it. But they could and did engage to the fullest extent in the economic possibilities allowed to those with business licenses—and paid taxes on earned income.

Women do show up in some guild records on an apparent visual par with men. That is, although not allowed to vote, their names appear in lists interspersed with the men's names—in lists dealing with monies collected and journeymen accepted, for instance. It is also clear that widows were allowed to accept and train apprentices, even long after their husbands had died. According to the 1801 census, Elisabeth Christine Berling, brewer and printer, had four apprentices and one journeyman listed in her household. Her husband had died in 1778, so these were hardly carryovers from his time. It is quite probable that married women in traditional "women's" businesses, such as millinery, could accept and train young women. Since there were no guilds in these fields, however, the traditional terms of "apprentice" and "journeyman" do not apply, nor are there extant records.

It is possible, indeed probable, that government willingness to extend business licenses to women may have been based partially on the desire to break guild monopolies, as well as to provide women with a way to support themselves. Separated or divorced women, for instance, regularly received permits enabling them to carry on in their ex-husbands' professions. Unlike widows, who were also allowed to continue husbands' businesses, granting licenses to divorcées increased the number of people working in a particular profession, since it is to be assumed that the ex-husband continued in his own business as well.

With the Lutheran Reformation in the sixteenth century, the Danish state inherited the Catholic church's responsibility for charity and care of the poor. A series of laws established regulations to care for the so-called "deserving poor," mostly widows and orphans. Able-bodied men were assumed to be able to care for themselves. Much of the responsibility for this care fell on local parishes, but governance of the royal residence city of Copenhagen was so intertwined with the state government that, in effect, the state had taken over poor care in Copenhagen, which it controlled through the Poor Commission. The more people who could support themselves, the fewer of them became the state's responsibility, so here government needs and guild demands clashed. Although the guild system was not formally abolished until the new Trade Law of 1857, the royal government had been chipping away at it for some time.

Another important law affecting women's legal position was the Danish concept of "unprobated property" (*uskiftet bo*), which allowed a widow to remain in and retain control of the family property until or unless she remarried. If there were children, they had to agree to this by themselves, if they were of age, or with guardians' consent if they were underage. Such situations were not uncommon, and wills often remained unprobated for years.[35] The subtext here is that widows were presumed to be competent and capable of continuing the family business. Indeed, if a woman survived childbirth, her chances of outliving her husband were great, so the actuality of women inheriting and managing husbands' businesses would have been a known circumstance. Girls in middle-class homes would have grown up knowing of this possibility, and it is quite clear that daughters did help in family businesses.

Methodology

Finding the women hidden in the archives posed a methodological challenge. About 250 women received licenses to own and run schools. Were there comparable numbers of women in other fields? Would census and citizenship records be a fruitful starting point? The problem with this approach is that, since the population of Copenhagen at the time of the 1801 census was around 100,000, going through all the census records would take a considerable amount of time. Additionally, since women were not granted citizenship, there would be no women in citizenship records. City directories offered another possible source. These were yearly printed alphabetical lists of people who lived in the city. Several women were included, sometimes with occupational titles, such as "Asbroek, silk dyeress," or "Bademejer, Mad[ame], polishes iron stoves," from the 1801 directory. Other women were listed as widows, as "Berling, brewer- and publisher-widow," but with no indication whether or not they were continuing in their deceased husband's business. Elisabeth Christine Berling did continue as both a brewer and a publisher, but did the Widow Blume, listed as "metalworker widow," continue as a metalworker?[36] Did any of these women have legal permission to carry on these trades, the defining qualification for my study? Since it was not possible to ascertain from the listings either the legality or the actuality of what these women may have been doing, city directories were used only as cross-references when women showed up elsewhere.

Instead, I scoured typed lists of material in the Copenhagen City Archives for potential sources. Discussions with archivists suggested additional sources; serendipity plays a major role in this type of research. Records of the Copenhagen City Council, boxes of business and travel licenses, lists of people given licenses to sell various goods in streets and markets, income tax records, and some guild records (for context) were all combed for women's names. This material was bolstered with individual property assessments as well as probate and bankruptcy records of specific individuals in the Danish National Archives. Records of the Danish Merchants Association from 1742 to 1835 in the National Business Archives in Århus (since moved to Viborg) were also checked, as was the police blotter from 1801.

I also cross-checked individual names with census records and city directories. Censuses listed a person's age, marital status, and the household make-up. Although generally considered to be accurate, neither the 1787 nor 1801 census was able to count everyone. These censuses depended very much on who physically showed up on the day of the census and on how people referred to themselves.[37] Since there were several census takers, categories and occupation designations, as well as spelling, were not always consistent. One needs to check several different spelling possibilities when looking for specific individuals. An additional problem with the Danish censuses that are available in searchable online databases comes under the category of human error. These records were manually typed into a database by people who could make simple typing mistakes and who could not always accurately read the old Danish handwriting.[38] When possible, it is best to check the original records, which have now been scanned in online. (Both the 1787 and the 1801 censuses have alphabetic registers, although these are not available online.) There was no census between 1801 and 1834, and unfortunately most of the 1834 census is missing. This makes it very difficult to track individuals into the nineteenth century. Copenhagen city directories, available for most years and scanned in online, do provide some information on the existence and addresses of individuals whose names one knows, but not on their household make-up.[39]

Business licenses (*næringsbreve, bevillinger*) were supposed to be issued by The 32 Men (the Copenhagen City Council) and most often were.

However, some licenses were also issued by royal authorities. The difference between the licenses issued by these two entities is not evident. Did refusal from one place send the applicant elsewhere? Could one appeal a municipal rejection to a royal authority? Were there different levels of understanding of the process? Practically, the existence of separate authorities means that the researcher has to check in several different places and that it will probably never be possible to find *all* the licenses issued.[40]

For the record, ninety-five women received royal privileges during the period under examination. Of these, about one-third were widows and one-third married. Of the remaining third, three were never married and three divorced; the marital status of the rest is unknown. This is not dramatically different from the overall percentages for women who received licenses, nor is there a different occupational distribution. In other words, there seems to be little or nothing that distinguishes recipients of royal privileges from those of "ordinary" communal licenses.

Moreover, the city government changed its organizational structure several times during this period. Until 1801, there was just one secretariat, led by a city clerk. From 1801 to 1805, there were four sections, each of which supposedly dealt with separate issues, but the reality seems to have been that their responsibilities overlapped considerably. After 1805, there were two secretariats. Additionally, *ad hoc* subcommittees were often formed.[41] All of this complicates the researcher's work and means that it will probably be impossible to capture all the appropriate information, but the overall picture would probably not be much changed, even if every license could be found.

One further point, not unusual for this period, is that records are often divided in several places. There is usually a kind of chronological diary listing all current issues. This diary then refers to other records or packets containing incoming and outgoing letters, licenses, or other material. Licenses, for example, were often supposed to be returned if the recipient was not going to use it or had finished using it. What this means is that material on the same subject, or regarding the same person, may be found scattered in several places, and one does not always have the complete story, as a part may be missing, never recorded, never returned, or simply lost.

The existence of several *ad hoc* subcommittees further tantalizes the researcher. In 1742, the city apparently decided that all the distilleries within the city boundaries needed to be inspected. The city clerk's office generated an extremely elaborate report of the 319 distilleries within the city of Copenhagen and on Christianshavn, based on individual inspections of each, with follow-up inspections six months later. But that was it. It was a one-time event; if it were done again, the records have not survived. For the record, there were fourteen women among the 319 distillers, all of them widows listed with their husbands' names.[42]

Similarly, in 1790, the city clerk's office generated a list of people who had licenses to trade in East Indian and West Indian goods. The list included about 250 names—all men; no women were listed.[43] Nonetheless, women did receive permission to trade in these foreign goods. In 1766, Anna Elisabeth Bihl (alternative spellings—Beil and Bail) received a royal privilege to travel to markets and sell various sorts of Asian textiles. Anna Bihl was married at the time to Jacob Preuser, whose occupation was not given.[44] Twenty-four years separate Anna's pass and the city document, but hers was not the only permission given. Maren Jensen was given permission in 1804 to sell Chinese and West Indian goods. Maren was divorced, with one son, and her former husband Søren Sødring was a distiller.[45] So what to make of this discrepancy? Was 1790 a year in which, completely arbitrarily, no women had permission to sell foreign goods? Did the recorder simply not see women, or were the passes so scattered that it was impossible to keep track of them all? Absences are always hard to prove, and here they must obviously be taken with several grains of salt. Explanations are easier when the list does include some women, as with the distillers.

At the other end of this time period, in 1817, the municipal tax collector (*Rodemester*) turned in a list of those not in compliance with the existing regulations regarding "junk dealers, ironmongers, auctioneers, restauranteurs, beer dispensers, tea and coffee shop owners, billiard parlor owners, market sellers, and small grocers." The list included eighteen women.[46] But here again, there is neither any previous listing, nor any future similar record.

I also checked boxes of guild records, such as the distillers guild. Women were not allowed to be formal guild members and there is no evidence that they were, although they obviously were allowed to carry out guild occupations and even train apprentices.

Oddly, one group of women did not turn up in any of this research, despite the certainty of their existence. These were school teachers and schoolkeepers. In doing research for an earlier book on private schools for girls in early modern Copenhagen, *Educating Middle Class Daughters: Private Girls Schools in Copenhagen, 1790-1820*, I found letters from about 250 women in Copenhagen who had applied for permission to establish schools.[47] These women did not show up in the other municipal documents because they came under the auspices of a separate municipal subcommittee, *Direktionen for Almue- og Borgerskolevæsenet* (the Copenhagen Board of Education). Might there be other groups equally missing from the general municipal records because they came under a separate subcommittee? Midwives, who come first to mind, had to be certified in order to practice, so most of them—approximately 500 during this period—have probably been found in the city records.

The lists and boxes concerning market passes turned out to be most fruitful. In fact, anyone interested in women's occupations during this time period might productively start with these documents. These were passes given to Copenhagen women to travel to markets and sell goods outside the city. They had nothing to do with the Copenhagen markets, because most of those sellers were not Copenhagen residents. Hundreds of these passes still exist and are available in the Copenhagen City Archives.[48] Although a couple of passes indicate travel as far as Århus or Ålborg, in Jutland, most are just for travel around Sjælland, the main island that is also home to Copenhagen. Some of these women were away for months at a time. From the extant passes, it is possible to chart the routes traveled, markets visited, and goods sold.

I created a database containing about 3,000 women who were economically active between 1740 and 1835. It includes entries for name, address, occupational title, occupational category, license or permit with date and source, travel permits with routes and conditions, property owned, taxes paid, birth and death dates, marital status, husband, and space for "additional information." This made it possible to sort for all married women, or all married women who paid taxes, or widows who dispensed beer, for example.

In order to put women's work into context, it was also necessary to understand what the men were doing. A couple of sources turned out to be of considerable use here. One was a list generated by the police department in 1806 of all the guilds in Copenhagen, with numbers of guild members and master craftsmen.[49] This list does not, of course, include all the men who worked in any given field; it does not, for example, include the free masters, nor men in fields not guild-controlled. And, of course, it includes no women. Still, for an indication of the kinds of occupations carried on in the capital city, with representative proportions, it is a very good source. It can also be compared with the guilds and occupations listed in the *Protocol of Municipal Offices*, a running list of all municipal civil servants from 1739 to 1805.[50] Together, these two sources can give the researcher an idea of the type and extent of work that was going on in preindustrial Copenhagen.

The other priceless source consisted of tax records. During this time period, the city of Copenhagen paid the royal government a semi-annual tax in lieu of quartering soldiers. Copenhagen was, after all, a military city. This tax was made up of two parts, a property tax and a self-employment tax. Records for the property tax, although the larger of the two, seem to have disappeared during this period, or maybe it was not collected. But, in any case, the self-employment tax records proved to be more useful, because they listed who was actually doing what and how much tax was paid. It is unknown how the amount of individual tax liability was determined, but the tax records seem to have followed the geography of the censuses; that is, people were listed by district and house or *matrikel*[51] number. The total amount of the tax paid by the city to the state government was fixed in advance and then divided into 2,000 portions. People were assessed, in some fashion, anywhere from one-quarter portion to six portions. In 1794, one portion was listed as 1 *rigsdaler*-5 *mark*-6 *skilling*.[52] However this tax was assessed, the point was that the end amount collected was fixed. Increasing one person's taxes would thus result in a decrease of someone else's—an eighteenth-century tax cap—not in an increase in total monies collected.

Records from 1801 were checked very thoroughly and then used in two different ways. There is a typed alphabetical register of all the names in the 1801 self-employment tax records (for use in genealogy research), which was checked for women's names in order to determine their jobs and how much tax they were assessed. Checking this register against the 1801 census would tell their ages and something about their family situations. Just over 80 percent of these women were in the census.

In order to help with context, I then analyzed the entire register from 1801. There are 6,207 people listed, with 93 percent men, 7 percent women. A list of all occupations was made and then grouped into categories—food, clothing, building trades, production (other than of clothing), service industries (including military and government jobs), shipping, and unknown. Since in a preindustrial economy, production and distribution were often done by the same person (the shoemaker both produced and then sold the shoes), these two functions were kept together. Categories were determined by the nature of the goods or products, not on the basis of their handling or distribution. Thus, everyone dealing with food was kept together in the "food" category, whether they sold raw vegetables or dispensed distilled liquor.

The biggest problem with categorizing occupations this way is that there was a large group of people engaged in the distribution of mixed, miscellaneous, and unknown goods, ranging from merchant ship owners to second-hand junk dealers. Merchants could be importing, transporting, and selling anything from raw sugar to finished cotton fabric, and, although junk dealers probably did not deal in food, their products could range from clothing to metal goods. These miscellaneous distributors have been included under production; when they are separated out, they totaled 330, of whom four were women. The following chart lists percentages of tax-payers but says nothing about the amounts paid. It is organized by category and gender.

Table 1.1

Total Self-Employment Tax-Payers

Category	Men	Women
Food	35%	27%
Services	18%	28%
Clothing	14%	5%
Production	12%	7%
Building Trades	9%	5%
Shipping	6%	2%
Unknown	6%	26%
Total	100%	100%

I am not sure this represents a dramatic difference in the percentages for men and women. Both sexes had about half of their tax-payers in the food and service industries, although there was a higher percent of men in the food industries than women. That is probably because "services" includes landlords, and a fairly high percent of women paid taxes on rents received. These would have been widows who inherited the family house but chose not to continue in the family business. Continuing to rent out rooms, apartments, or floors would have been relatively easy. The women in these records were all widows; tax collectors followed the census records, so if there had been a man in the household, he was the one on whom taxes would have been levied. Women paid these taxes only if there were no man around.

In this way, one can get a sense for the kinds of jobs the state thought generated enough income on which to collect taxes and for how the occupations split between men and women. Since this was a self-employment tax, it did not include anyone who was salaried or who worked for someone else. Nor, it became obvious, did it include those people (mostly women?) who made so little money as not to be worth taxing, such as market women or women who peddled yarn, thread, or candles. Since the total amount of tax to be collected was fixed in advance, it did not make sense to collect from people who earned little money. (See Appendix 3.1 for a list of all the occupational categories, divided by sex.)

The sources checked were all official records. The women documented there all either understood the system well enough to be able to apply for the requisite permits (or knew someone who understood the system well enough to apply on their behalf), or made enough money to show up on a financial radar screen. What of all the other women who worked with no legal permission, who existed on the margins, in the shadows, or completely underground in a black market? We know they existed, for they have always existed. There is no reason to suppose this period would be any different. By their very nature, though, shadow, grey, and black economies hide from the light and are difficult to expose. They might show up in police or court records. Indeed, police records were checked but did not prove to be a fruitful source. Out of a total of 5,022 entries in the Copenhagen police blotter for the single year of 1801, only thirty-seven dealt with issues that might conceivably have relevance for this study. These were mostly women who were turned in or cited for offering goods "of a suspicious nature" for sale.[53]

Nonetheless, a positive case can be made for limiting this study to those women who had legal permissions. If one is researching women who were in business for themselves, then the very legality of their occupations proves that they were not necessarily *femmes couvertes*. The openness of their positions helps to support the idea that women were allowed to function on their own. These women were not hiding, not operating in the shadows or on the margins, but rather carrying on their businesses in the full light of day. It is not necessary to highlight illegal activity in order to find legal activity.

But even with official records, some issues still need to be discussed. First, the records are rather episodic. Very few of the sources have a nice chronological trajectory. Some have only one entry, while others start and then stop and maybe pick up years later. What the records contain depends somewhat on the interest of the government and somewhat on the interest and enthusiasm of the record keeper. Johan Thomas Flindt, for instance, who was the City Clerk in 1794 (a rather elevated position, as he lists his title as "mayor"), wrote an extremely detailed account of the running of the city. It was a sort of how-to manual on city government, with a lot of material on city finances.[54] Someone in the city government kept a running list of civil servants, ranging from "The 32 Men," to the night soil collectors. This list stretches from 1739 to 1805, but not all record keepers were equally enthusiastic or energetic.[55]

Another problem is the sheer absence of some records. The city of Copenhagen burned three times during this period, in 1728, 1795, and 1807. Many records were lost in these fires. And during the Second World War, the Germans apparently used boxes of archival material for target practice—better, one readily admits, than using people, but it does cause problems for the researcher.

Taken together, this means that it is possible neither to create a complete set of static pictures nor the historian's preferred change over time. What emerges is a series of snapshots, incomplete and sometimes blurry, which can not be forced together into a coherent whole but rather provide a crazy quilt of activities and possibilities. Nor is it possible to follow an entire life, or even the adult working life, of any of these women. Even for wealthy women who left the most records, there are often gaps in the biographies. Elisabeth Christine Berling (1744-1801) comes to mind. As a publisher from a publishing family, there is an unusual amount of extant printed material, but still not her whole story. This is frustrating for the reader, as well as the researcher. We *want* to know the whole story. But rather than trying to fill in the unknown parts, I have chosen to leave them empty and to weave around the open spaces.

There are two ways to approach this material—either by discussing women in their familial roles, such as widowed or married, or by discussing women in various industries or occupations. I have chosen the latter approach, not only because women's familial roles changed over time, although we know it only at one particular moment, but also because it gave greater coherence to the narrative not to be skipping around through social classes and occupations. The women have been divided into three general groups, with one chapter devoted to each group. The first group includes those women at the bottom of the social scale, those whose occupations kept them outside, on the streets (not including "street walkers"), women who peddled small amounts of goods on streets and in markets. These women made so little money that they rarely, if ever, show up in tax records. They were supposed to have permits, however, so the trajectory of their lives did intersect with an official bureaucracy at some point. That there were other women who never came to official attention is obvious, but they are not the subject of this study.

The second group of women also worked at street level, but they worked from inside fixed structures rather than outside on the streets. These would be small shopkeepers, restauranteurs, schoolkeepers, and dressmakers. They worked from within what we today would call "brick and mortar" structures (distinguishing them from virtual business), but what the eighteenth century referred to as "brick and timber" structures. Operating from within solid structures, these were middle-class women who ran the gamut from petty bourgeois to wealthy upper middle class.

And finally, there was a small group of women who owned large-scale businesses. Unlike the retail shopkeeper, these women owned sizable merchant houses, ships, and manufactories. In contrast to the other two groups, these women were mostly, although not exclusively, widows. In a society that still had a nobility, these women were technically not upper class, but they did hobnob with the nobility and often controlled as much, if not more, money than did the titled nobility.

As can be seen, women worked throughout the economy. The idea that women were not gainfully employed outside the home is a construct of the Victorian era, which wished to push women back into their homes in an attempt to impose a concept of domesticity on the entire society. Victorian prescriptions outran the reality even then, but later generations came to believe that women did indeed remain within the confines of a domestic home. Later, when twentieth-century historians began looking for working women, they had difficulty finding them. There are several possible reasons for the apparent disappearance of women from urban economies. One is, of course, that many women did work inside their homes. Another is that women were often subsumed within their husbands' official and archival records. But I believe there is another equally compelling possibility. Since women were to be found everywhere, their presence was not a notable event. We notice and comment on the exceptional, not the ordinary. So the failure to observe and report working women can also mean that it was an unexceptional everyday occurrence. Their apparent invisibility is thus a product of the constructed layers of veils through which we are looking for them.

These, then, are the stories of women who worked in their own names—women who ran businesses, peddled goods, produced wares, and lived their lives in the preindustrial city of Copenhagen. Some did quite well, owned large businesses and fancy houses that they passed on to children; others barely eked out a living, peddling on the streets of the city. But all of them worked for themselves, and their families, and they did not disappear into the occupations of husbands, sons, brothers, or fathers. They were the authors of their own stories. They worked and survived as women.

Chapter Two

On the Streets and in the Markets

Gundel Maria Munk, widowed and left with three small children by the time she was thirty-two, used her husband's license as a drysalter to travel from Copenhagen and sell linen, hemp, and dried salted fish products at provincial markets on the island of Sjælland. In 1786, she requested permission from the Copenhagen city authorities to allow her journeyman, Tobias Ritzow, to accompany her on these trips. Fifteen years later, in 1801, Tobias was still listed in Gundel Maria's household, still as a journeyman. Her young son, Jacob (now aged twenty-two), was also listed as a journeyman, and the household had a new "boy" in addition to Jacob and Tobias, also in residence. Tobias, now forty-three, never became a master nor did he receive his own license as a drysalter.[1] Nor did he marry Gundel. For whatever reason, Gundel Maria continued to function in her own name as a drysalter; she remained listed as the head of household with authority to accept and train apprentices and to retain them as journeymen in her household.

In 1816, Lene Tønder applied for permission to sit on a city street and sell domestic fruit. She had been doing this for thirty-seven years but had just discovered that she needed official permission. She was fifty-two, single, "sickly and weak," and claimed she was not healthy enough to "earn my upkeep with work." So as "not to be a burden to the Poor Commission," she applied to continue as a street seller. She lived at no. 30 Skindergade, in Copenhagen, in the cellar.[2]

Dorothea Müller, who continued to function as a "French bread baker" after her husband Caspar's death, apparently got tired of writing individual references for each of the women who bought bread from her, so she sent one inclusive list to the city authorities. Guild bakers were wholesalers; the retailing of bread was done by individuals who needed city permits to peddle bread legally on the streets. In order to receive such a permit, the applicant had to show that she bought from an authorized guild baker and was reputable. Müller "took the liberty to remark that they [the applicants] were all poor people, most of them have extensive families whom they support in this manner, thus not becoming a burden to the public." Müller's list included twenty women, aged twenty-five to eighty, half of whom were widowed, eight were married, while the marital status of the remaining two was not given. Overwhelmingly, these women claimed to have anywhere from two to seven underage children at home whom they were supporting. Even a "seventy-five-year-old" woman was listed as having two children. It is not clear whose children these were.

Obviously her own children would be adults by now. Perhaps these were grandchildren, or the children of other relations or friends. The list is not clear; it just claims that these children were her responsibility.[3]

What these women had in common is that they were all at the tail end of a preindustrial urban distribution system. They sold small quantities of food and clothing, most of which they had not produced themselves but rather had bought for resale. These women were not at the very bottom of the social structure, but only slightly above it. They were women who struggled to survive, yet mostly managed. They were a large part of the mechanism for the distribution of goods, not only within the capital city of Copenhagen, but also throughout the country, as they traveled miles across Denmark, often for months at a time, peddling goods. This chapter tells their stories. These are stories of active female agency. Not only did these women function throughout the urban economy, they were so ubiquitous that they were neither unusual nor surprising.

Through both the good years of the late eighteenth century, during the early Napoleonic War years and the Danish alliance with Napoleon, and the bad years after Denmark declared bankruptcy in 1813, these women continued to peddle their wares. The economic crash brought on by Denmark's unsuccessful involvement in the Napoleonic Wars and the demobilization following the war had an impact on people throughout the economy. There was much talk of "hard times," and "in these economic times," but people continued to need to eat and to require the services of a distribution system. Jobs may have been tougher to find, but licenses continued to be issued and taxes to be paid.

These women took active charge of their own lives. No matter how bad the times or difficult their positions, they made conscious choices and decisions about their futures. They did not just happen into jobs or acquiesce in bad situations. The very process of applying to a municipal or royal authority for permission to act in a certain capacity underlines their conscious actions. They were capable of functioning on their own in order to support themselves and often their families as well. Whether they were selling bread on the streets or traveling to markets across the Danish countryside, they made active choices about their own lives.

They were also "well-behaved" women whose contact with government authorities at all levels was legal. They applied for and received business permits and licenses; they paid taxes; they followed the laws and regulations. In short, they were doing precisely what they were supposed to do. Either they themselves possessed a fair amount of bureaucratic literacy, which enabled them to negotiate government bureaucracy, or they knew how to find someone else who could, which also implies a certain amount of bureaucratic know-how. They may have engaged in illegal or marginal activities as well, but their appearance in city records was all aboveboard.

This chapter uses official records of legal activities to get at what women were doing. Both the royal Danish government and the city of Copenhagen kept extensive records of applications for business licenses and permits, as well as tax and guild records. The city of Copenhagen was quite meticulous in recording all requests for permits to produce, import, or sell goods, as well as the disposition of these requests. This, then, is a picture of independent working women in eighteenth- and early nineteenth-century preindustrial Copenhagen. These women had autonomous interactions with authorities in their own names, not in the names of husbands, fathers, sons, or brothers. In about half the cases, the women involved were married, but they nonetheless still acted on their own.

Street Vendors

Street vendors were probably one of the most obvious categories of women workers—they were literally on the streets where they could be seen. They sold their wares from street stalls, doorways, windows, cellar doors, on squares and under bridges. People in early modern urban economies could not live a subsistence lifestyle; they were forced onto the market to acquire everyday necessities such as food and clothing. Much food was bought prepared or semi-prepared from street-sellers who hawked their wares on the city streets. People who lived in small one- or two-room apartments rarely had kitchens, which were the province of wealthier homes, and hence had no place to cook or prepare food.[4] Food could be heated on whatever kind of stove was used for heating or cooked in an oven in someone else's kitchen, such as at a bakery, but much was simply bought ready-to-eat on the streets. Overwhelmingly, this food was sold by women such as Lene Tønder.

Vendors were supposed to have permits in order to sell food on the streets. A permit gave access to a specific spot—on the street, in an alley, in a cellar opening. Rental for this spot was paid either to the city, if it were on the streets, or to the building owner, if the space were on private property. Copenhagen pedestrians were not always amenable to the sale of food on the streets. K.H. Seidelin, who edited *Politivennen* (The Police Friend), was not happy about a woman selling produce on Østergade, in downtown Copenhagen. On January 10, 1801, Seidelin complained:

> On Østergade, at the corner of Kristenbernikovstræde, a *green-groceress* [*Grønkone*] uses not only a stall, but also the cellar. No matter how much one objects to the stall on the sidewalk, which is barely two feet wide, it is even worse when a greengrocer, as here, lets her cellar door stand continually open, as that completely blocks all passage on the paving stones. Rather than making it easy for pedestrians to make their way around her by closing the cellar door, she has presumptuously had the temerity to fasten it open with a lock.[5]

A week later, she had stopped locking her door open, but Seidelin still was not happy:

> The *greengroceress* on the corner of Kristenbernikovstræde and Østergade has stopped locking her cellar door open (but she still opens it and thereby blocks the sidewalk; by providing hinges on the edges protruding into the sidewalk, the inconvenience would be eliminated.)[6]

Of course, the greengroceress was engaging in the well-used tactic of trying to attract potential customers. If people had to go out of their way to walk around her stall, they might just stop and buy something. Seidelin was not sympathetic.

From 1796 through 1816, the Copenhagen city government received 778 applications from women to sell bread on the city streets. Overwhelmingly, these women were already peddling their wares on the streets. The number of statements that they already were buying from guild bakers attests to this, and every application includes such a statement. So, what these applications actually represent were not requests to sell bread, but rather attempts to regularize or legalize an already-existing situation. This probably represents just a small percentage of the total number of bread sellers; it is impossible to know how many other women never had contact with the authorities. Some applications quite candidly state that the applicant had no idea she needed a permit until she was stopped by the police. Most women simply wrote of their own troubles, of "these difficult times," of sick or weak relatives and several underage children at home to support. Lene Tønder, as we saw, wanted to support herself and not become a burden on the Poor Commission.[7]

That times were hard hardly accounted for the fact that every woman seemed to have several underage children to support and that all the married women wrote of sick, weak, or otherwise incapacitated husbands. One should probably not take the specifics of their application stories too literally. The times were indeed "hard," but having several underage children was probably known to be a sure way of receiving a permit. This could either be because of a growing belief in "domesticity"—the idea that women were supposed to take care of the home and children—or a simple expedient for making sure that care of women and children did not devolve on the city or state. In either, or both, cases, having children to support facilitated the receipt of a street-selling permit, or so women believed or were told.[8]

Ninety-one women applied for street licenses in the single year of 1816. Of these, thirty-six were married, thirty-one were widowed, while the marital status of the remaining twenty-four is unknown. Married women's husbands, and thus the women, were overwhelmingly from the artisan class, *sans culottes*. Ten husbands were listed as "workers" (*arbejdsmand*—an acknowledged job title, which was often military), eight were definitely in the military, and the remainder included a variety of journeymen and "free master" carpenters, shoemakers, and tailors. However, the reason usually given for a married woman's application was that her husband was no longer able to work. Nicolaj Lundoph Hanekiær, a free master tailor, applied on June 5, 1816, on behalf of his wife, stating that "[i]n these hard times, it is impossible for me to sustain myself and my family, since I am a cripple and must use two crutches. I therefore apply for a stall where my wife may sit and sell bread."[9]

Passes, once issued, gave the holder permission to sell specific goods, in a specific spot. Sellers were not supposed to wander, nor to enter into people's houses uninvited. Dorothea Devitz drew a very careful map, showing exactly where she intended to sell her goods and included permission from the shopkeeper in front of whose shop she would sit. Dorothea was fifty-six; her husband, Friedrich, was in the military, but they were not allowed to trade "in the barracks," although no reason was given for this. They had eight children, five still at home.[10]

There is a certain pathos to these applications. Although it is obvious from the handwriting that hired scribes wrote several of the applications, many women wrote their own. One can almost see a woman, suddenly confronted by a government official, sitting in a small room somewhere, laboriously writing an application. The handwriting is often shaky, hesitant, childish in its form, written by someone who is neither used to nor comfortable with the process of writing. Such an example is Anne Christine Sivertzen's 1807 application to sit and sell bread outside the prison on Christianshavn. She had permission from the prison warden to do so. Sivertzen wrote the top part; the bottom was written by Andr. Schreibe, obviously more comfortable with writing, attesting to the fact that Anne Christine bought 4 *skilling* worth of wheat (white) bread daily, presumably from him.[11]

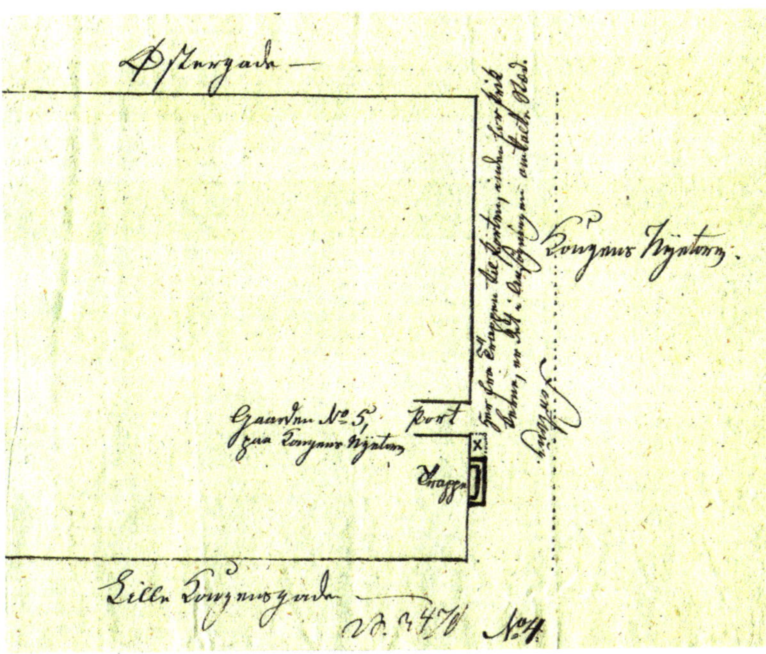

Figure 2.1. Dorothea Devitz's application to sell bread on Kongens Nytorv. Københavns Magistrat, Stadesedler, no. 755/1816, Copenhagen City Archives.

To get permission to sell bread, these women had to prove that they had access to guild-approved bakers from whom to buy. Most of the applications, therefore, included a statement from a guild baker that the applicant was a "respectable" (*skikkelig*) woman who had bought bread from them for several years. Applications often included statements from landlords attesting to the length of time the applicant had lived at their place, thus proving her "stability." Several of these statements from bakers were signed by women, mostly bakers' widows, such as Dorothea Müller, but women, nonetheless. Obviously some women (widows) had the legal standing to testify in support of other women.[12]

Military wives made up another large group of women food vendors. It was well known that military pay was not enough to support a family. An ordinance of July 27, 1742, gave military wives permission to sell fruit,

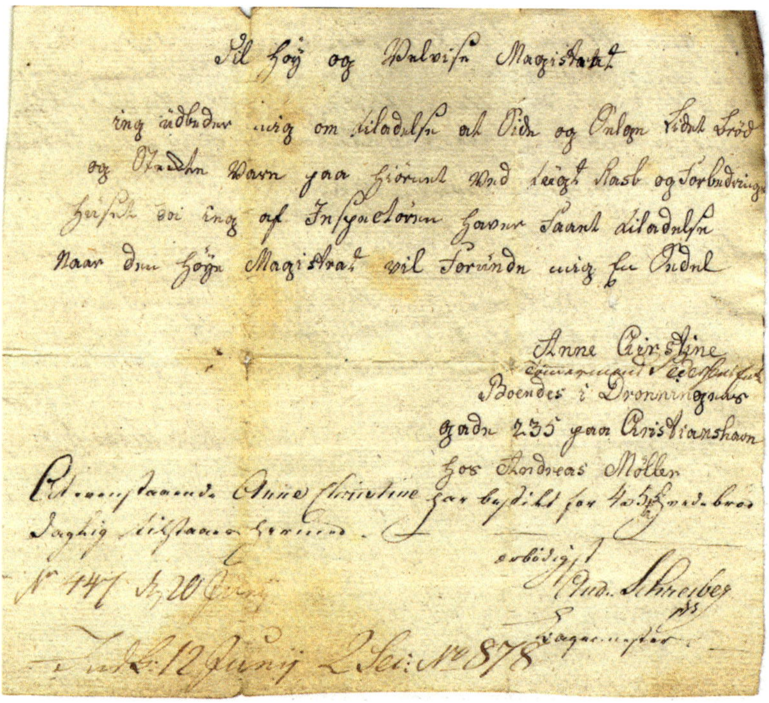

Figure 2.2. Anne Christine Sivertzen's application to sell bread. Københavns Magistrat, *Stadesedler*, no. 447/1807, Copenhagen City Archives.

oysters, fish, and lemons on the street. This replaced earlier laws, which, it was feared, had allowed women to sell fenced goods. Presumably, this new law would regularize the economic activities of military wives. Permits were issued to 670 military women between 1773 and 1819. Of these, only twenty-seven were widows and one was single.[13]

These were the two largest groups of women street vendors. Of the approximately 3,000 women in my database, roughly half were selling goods on the streets. There is evidence of at least the following types of legal vendors.

Table 2.1

Copenhagen Women Street Vendors

Sellers of bread, occasionally fruit and cakes	778
Sellers of fruit, oysters, fish, and lemons (military wives)	670
Sellers of used clothing	97
Sellers of thread and yarn	64
Sellers of unspecified goods	18
Total	1,627

There may have been more, indeed there probably were others, but this represents the minimum numbers, since a name and address can be attached to each one.

Of the women who peddled used clothing, about half were married and a quarter widowed. There is no information available on the remaining quarter. Husbands, when there is any information about them, came from the same group of artisans as did those whose wives sold bread on the streets. Anne Cathrine Olsen received a license from the city of Copenhagen on May 24, 1809, to sell used clothing. She was also informed that she was not allowed to hang her wares outside the house where she lived. If she could not sell her goods from within her apartment, then the city would assign her a spot.[14] The regulations for dry goods vendors echoed those for food sellers. It would not do to have vendors roaming the streets, accosting potential customers, and disrupting the activities of good citizens, something of which Seidelin often complained. The city government tried to maintain uninhibited passage on the streets and a buyer-friendly environment.

Among the more moving of these licenses were those that went to women who peddled yarn, thread, and sometimes candles on the streets. One cannot help wondering how much income this could possibly provide. Of the roughly one-third who were widows, the licenses make it quite clear that sufficient support was an expectation, as these women's licenses were conditional on their remaining unmarried. K.M. Dein, Kristina Grimlund, Lise Hartvig, and Else Marie Mørck all received such licenses in exchange for surrendering their late husbands' citizenship papers (*borgerbreve*). Their husbands had all had middle-class jobs. Dein had been a butcher, Grimlund an innkeeper, Hartvig a merchant, and Mørck a distiller. So selling thread and yarn on the streets would represent a considerable downward slide for these women. But this was in the 1830s when times were bad. Maybe the husbands' businesses had not been doing well, or their widows just felt incapable of carrying on the family business.

Husbands of married women applying to peddle goods on the street often had dependable jobs. Among husbands, there were a tailor, a ropemaker, a buttonmaker, a baker, a master blacksmith, a couple of journeymen carpenters, and ship captains (who, admittedly, might be gone for long periods of time). Severine Hansen, whose husband was a ship captain, received a two-year license to peddle yarn, thread, candles, and rye bread. This was obviously an attempt to tide her over during her husband's absences. Rikke Furst, whose husband dealt in woolen and linen goods, was given a license to sell "while her husband was gone." It is unclear if her husband traveled in order to sell his goods, which is probable, or that he had simply disappeared and this was to help her out until his reappearance. In any case, the Copenhagen powers-that-be viewed peddling thread and yarn as a means to make a sufficient income to keep women off the poor rolls, if still on the streets.[15]

Market Selling

Copenhagen, like most European cities, held regular fixed markets. Copenhagen held its markets on Wednesdays and Saturdays. These were meant to be places where peasants from outside the city could sell their wares to city residents. They sold from fixed stands and rolling carts, which were leased to sellers by the city. Copenhagen residents were not allowed to sell goods in competition to those offered by non-residents. City dwellers were allowed to buy in the early morning from these markets only for their own use. At ten in the morning, the red market flag came down, however, and markets were opened to anyone. Street vendors could then buy goods legally for retail resale. That many vendors also bought goods illegally before the market flag came down is also true; this was one of the more common complaints registered in the 1801 Copenhagen police blotter.[16]

The several markets in central Copenhagen were divided by products. On Gammel Torv and Nytorv, outside the Town Hall, peasants sold grain, eggs, butter, peas, geese, sides of pork, poultry, and other larded goods. On Amagertorv and Højbroplads, one could buy vegetables and fruit. Fisherwomen sold from stands on Gammelstrand, while butchers could be found on Ulfeldts Plads (modern day Gråbrødretorv) and in front of Nikolaj Church. All of these goods came from outside the city walls. Peasants and city residents were not supposed to compete over the sale of the same goods.[17]

Although not allowed to sell goods at the Copenhagen markets, another group of women traveled from the city to rural provincial markets and peddled their wares outside the city. They were itinerant peddlers who sold their wares at booths in fixed markets, rather than from wandering wagons. The regulations in late eighteenth- and early nineteenth-century Copenhagen stipulated that one needed a "market pass" if one wanted to leave the city to sell at provincial markets. These passes were issued by Copenhagen city officials and gave permission to travel on a specific date to a specific place, usually following a specified route.[18] The traveler would then present her pass to city officials in the stipulated town; they, in turn, would issue her a permit to sell at their market. Often the seller had to rent a booth at the market as well. After the market, the seller would then be issued another pass to the next market in another town a day or two later. There the process would start again. Market sellers were often gone for weeks or months at a time before they returned home to Copenhagen. Gundel Maria Munk traveled on such a pass. For Copenhageners, this was the reverse of their home markets. In both cases, it was *non*-residents who sold goods to residents in the market place. This would tend to limit competition in any one place and to establish different sales places for different people based on residency.

Market sellers were supposed to save all these passes and return them to city officials when they returned to Copenhagen. Sometimes there were several sets of passes, while other times a single sheet of paper, endorsed and endorsed again, over and over, sufficed. There are twenty-two boxes of these returned passes in the Copenhagen City Archives, covering the period from 1778 to 1826; passes were issued to a total of 649 individuals.[19] Slightly less than 10 percent of these passes were issued to women. Obviously, one cannot assume that these were *all,* or even the only, people who traveled to sell at provincial markets. The returned passes would only indicate the most organized and legal travelers. That passes were lost en route, never returned, or never obtained in the first place cannot be discounted. There are enough extant passes, nonetheless, to draw conclusions about the nature of the process.

A more important caveat is that the authorities were rarely consistent in how they recorded information on passes. Women were sometimes listed under their husband's male name, even though the husband had died, sometimes as his widow, and sometimes just as "Mrs. So-and-So." So marital status cannot be assumed from the information on passes. When the status is stated, it has been verified through some other documentation, such as census records. No marital status was listed for roughly 40 percent of the women; of the remaining 60 percent, slightly

Chart 2.1

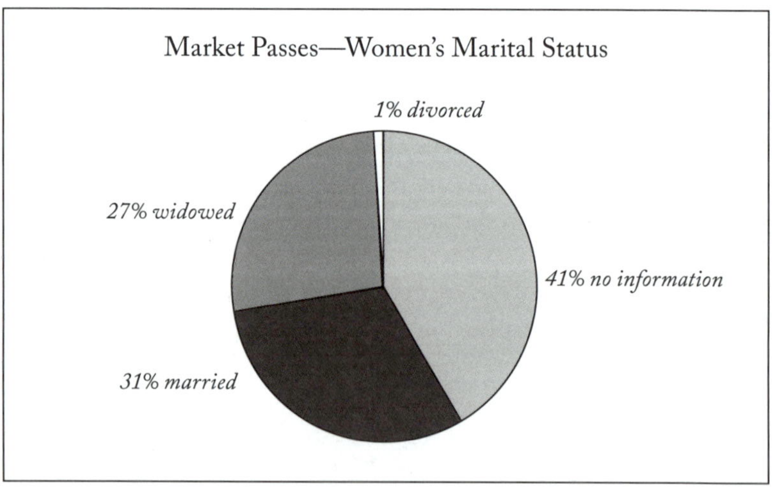

over half were married and just under half were widowed. Two women were divorced. Of the married women, approximately one-third either traveled with their husbands or sold goods that their husbands either worked with or imported. But another third sold goods that had no relation to their husband's work or trade—the wives of the landscape painter, the goldsmith, the customs official, and the groundskeeper, for example, peddled goods far removed from their husbands' jobs. For the remaining third of the married women, no information was given on their husbands' occupations.

At least 103 women received market passes during this period.[20] Overwhelmingly, women sold clothing and fabric; this constituted 70 percent of the passes. The remaining 30 percent sold some form of baked goods and a variety of miscellaneous items ranging from soap and perfume to rope, copper, and tin.[21] Gundel Maria Munk, as we know, peddled dried fish, linen, and hemp. Karen Søholm received a travel pass on September 10, 1819, to trade in baked goods, fruit, and cakes. She was a widow, whose husband had been a brewer. Her route took her to Frederiksborg, Slagelse, Fredensborg, and Roskilde—about 150 miles. She continued to travel through 1826.[22] Considering the length of some of these trips, often hundreds of miles, and the time spent en route, which could stretch to several months, nonperishable or long-lasting goods must have been a necessity. Additionally, the sale of fresh produce would probably have been restricted to local growers.

Most of the clothing sold consisted of decorations and accessories for women, followed by women's and children's clothing, mostly made or sewn by the women who sold them. This represents a departure from the more common pattern of women acting as intermediaries and selling items that they had not themselves produced. Maren Bay, a widow, received a license from the royal government on May 14, 1784, to sell hats, scarves, and children's clothing that she had sewn or knitted herself. Her travels took her around Sjælland to Helsingør, St. Hedinge, Næstved, Roskilde, Køge, Slagelse, and Frederiksborg, about 200 miles. She made these trips, looping back and forth following market days, for at least twenty-two years.[23]

Kirstine Adams, who traveled with her husband Adam Hansen's citizenship papers from 1741 to sell "grocer goods," went to nineteen separate markets on Sjælland during the three-month period of September through November in 1778. All told, there are thirty-four separate passes

Table 2.2

Market Passes for Women, 1778–1826

Clothing	Decorations (*damepynt*)	26
	Hats, scarves, etc.	17
	Women's clothing	9
	Children's clothing	7
	Stockings	4
	Old clothes	3
	Shoes	2
	Total Clothing	68
Fabric	Needlework	7
	Linen, wool	4
	Printed cloth, calico	3
	Wool carders	2
	"Woven"	1
	Total Fabric	17
Food	Baked goods	14
	Fruit	1
	Grocer goods	1
	Total Food	16
Other	Toys, dolls	8
	Cooper, tin	3
	Used goods/junk	3
	Oil, soap, perfume	2
	Hardware	1
	Jugs	1
	Boxes	1
	Rope	1
	Total Other	20
	Total passes	**121**

Source: Københavns Magistrat, 2. sekretariat, "Markedspasser, tilbageleverede," 1778-1826; "Protokol over Markedspasser." Copenhagen City Archives.

written out to Kirstine Adams. These listed a variety of fabric and cloth goods and materials, explaining which she could and could not sell. One pass indicated that she was allowed to take with her anything not sold at a particular market and to try sell it at the next market. Several of the passes were written on and endorsed several times

Passes listed the goods the passholder was allowed to sell, and sometimes also goods that the holder was prohibited from selling. Such prohibitions were often occasioned when the passholder could not prove the origin of her goods or whether her goods were bought from an authorized (i.e., guild) seller. Johanna Gianelli, married to Dominicus Gianelli, received a pass on April 26, 1773, to sell "domestic manufactured goods." Her husband also had a pass, from 1768, to trade in Chinese and East Indian goods. Johanna's pass, however, stipulated that she was not allowed to sell five and a half dozen glasses of "smelling water" (*lugtende vand* = perfume or smelling salt water?) and sixteen dozen Italian flowers. This is clearly very specific, so it probably referred to goods she already had but whose origins she could not prove. Her pass, again, was for travel around Sjælland—Roskilde, Korsør, Hillerød, Vordingborg, Slagelse, Næstved and Helsingør—maybe 300 miles. The anomaly here is that her husband had permission to travel with her. Passes were sometimes issued to her, sometimes to him, and sometimes to both. One pass was actually issued to "Dominicus Gianelli, shopkeeperess [female form] (*kræmmerske*)."[24] What can one make of this? Probably that scribes could also be inaccurate and inconsistent in the eighteenth century. At any rate, Johanna continued to travel at least until 1787, although she made only one trip that year, a practice that had begun a couple of years earlier. The Gianellis were not particularly poor; in 1771, Dominicus paid a three-quarter portion in property taxes, which means they probably owned a building in Copenhagen.[25]

Although most women received passes to travel around Sjælland, a small group traveled to Odense on the island of Fyn, Århus, and even Ålborg on the Jutland peninsula. There does not seem to be any appreciable difference in what they were selling, so it is assumed that their destinations depended on personal preferences and personal connections. Cathrine Kaufmann made several trips to Århus and Ålborg between 1815 and 1825, using a pass from 1812 to sell ladies' decorations. She was married to Georg Gotfred Kaufmann, a master tailor.[26]

It is quite obvious that selling at various provincial markets was important business; it engaged many people. Four female market vendors

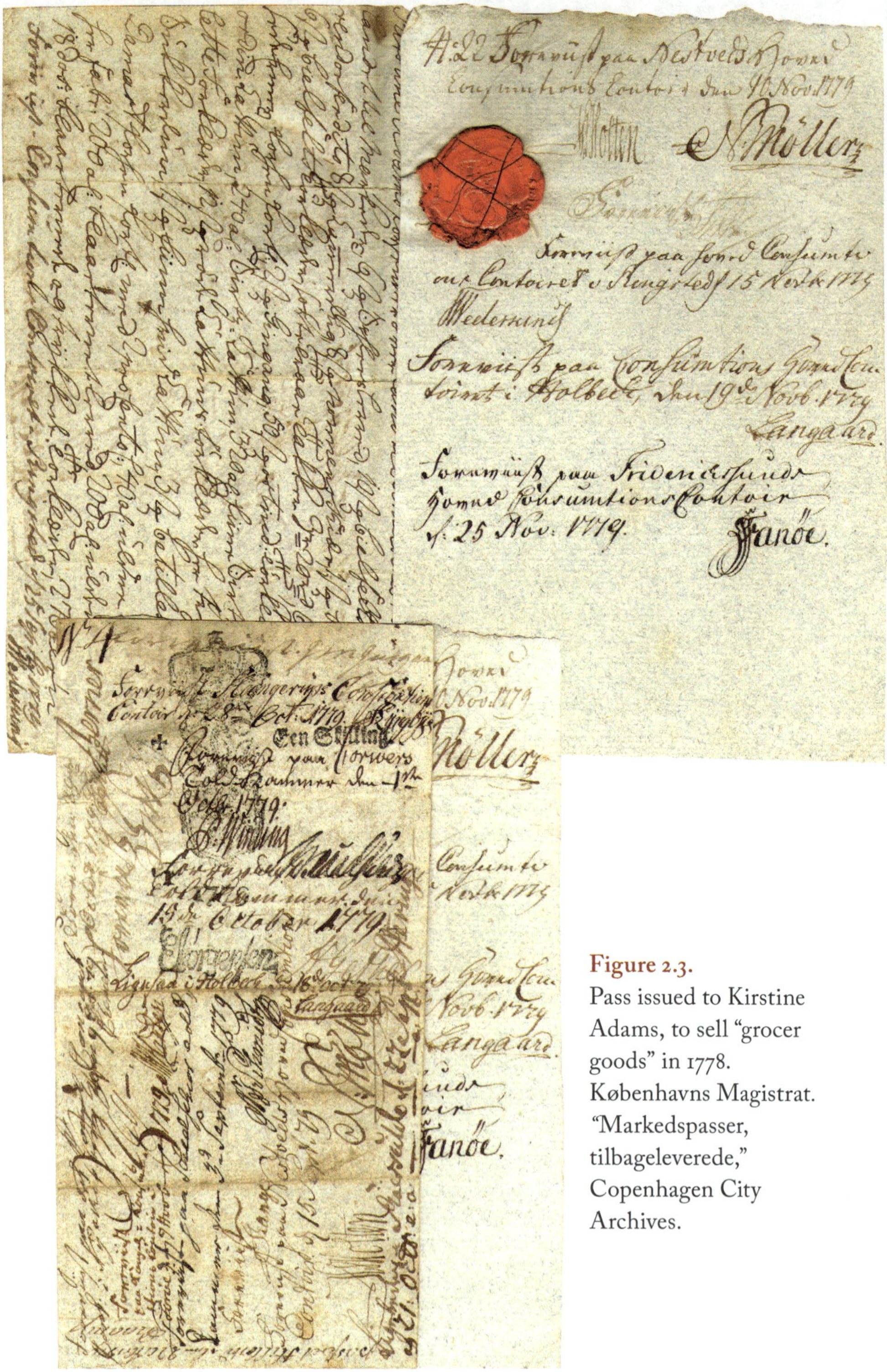

Figure 2.3.
Pass issued to Kirstine Adams, to sell "grocer goods" in 1778. Københavns Magistrat. "Markedspasser, tilbageleverede," Copenhagen City Archives.

actually paid self-employment taxes in 1771, ranging from a quarter to one and a quarter portions, and in 1801, three women paid taxes ranging from a quarter to one whole portion.[27] The simplest reason that women did not show up more frequently on self-employment tax records is probably that they did not make enough income to be worth bothering about for this particular tax, which was capped at a prespecified amount. Including more tax-payers would not have increased tax revenue, but would rather have created more work for tax collectors.

There were probably also traveling salespeople from other places in Sjælland, as well as locals offering goods at the various markets. The papers available in the Copenhagen City Archives only include passes for Copenhagen residents, not for residents of other cities. This reflected the end of a distribution system that in some cases started with the buying of imported goods from ship owners or shipping agents, went through wholesalers, and sometimes retailers as well, to the individual saleswoman. It was also the end of a system that could involve domestic production of various products, such as clothing, toys, and women's apparel. In such cases, the women served both as the producers and as the vendors, as did Karen Mariager, for example, who traveled selling the rope produced in her shop.

The women in this chapter were all active participants in their own lives. Whether through planned decisions or the vagaries of fate, they took control of their situations and acted in a fashion to enable them to continue to survive. Through good times and bad, they devised strategies to cope, not just for themselves, but in many cases also for children and even husbands. They were an integral part of an early modern distribution system and, as such, were necessary to the early modern urban economy of Copenhagen.

Chapter Three

Brick and Timber: Distribution, Production, and Services

Women selling on the streets and in the markets were a visible part of the urban economy. Somewhat less visible, but just as important, another group of women plied their trades from within solid structures, buildings built of brick and timber, the eighteenth-century equivalent of the twenty-first-century's "brick and mortar" shops. These women sold merchandise, produced goods, and offered services, all from within fixed structures. They were "solid," in both meanings of the term; the structures were built to last—indeed, some still do—and the businesses flourished. They included everything from grocery stores and restaurants, through milliners and publishers, to midwives and schoolkeepers. All these women were in business for themselves. Married, widowed, and single, they sometimes started their own businesses, and sometimes continued those of their husbands, but at the time they had contact with a government official, they were in charge of their own businesses. This chapter is divided in three parts: food distribution and service; production, which often includes distribution of the goods produced; and other services.

Food Distribution and Service

Roughly half of the women in my database were involved in the food industry in some fashion. The previous chapter discussed women who sold from stalls on the streets and in marketplaces, but women also sold groceries from within fixed buildings. At least sixty-five women did business as retail grocers. Twenty of these paid self-employment taxes, either one-quarter or one-half portion, which was not much. Mostly these women sold fruits and vegetables, spices, and other "colonial goods," which originally referred to goods from tropical colonial climes but eventually came to mean most kinds of dry, non-perishable foods. People in this business were typical retailers, who received permission to sell goods in small quantities directly to consumers. These small grocers (*hørkræmmere* or *høkere*) were organized in a guild. According to a police report from 1806, the grocers guild had forty-one masters, thirty-six journeymen, and forty apprentices—all men, naturally. Interestingly, though, five years earlier, in 1801, 325 men had paid some self-employment tax as small grocers, so a large number of men were working as grocers outside of the guilds. Women were roughly 6 percent of the tax-paying small grocers, also outside the guild structure.

Titles for people involved in retailing were fluid. The smallest shops were those organized in the *hørkræmmere* guild, which also included *høkere* (hawkers, sellers of very small quantities of goods). People listed as *købmand* (grocer, retailer) generally had larger businesses, sometimes shading into the category of *grosserere*, merchants or wholesalers. Merchants were not organized into a guild, although they did have a voluntary association, started in 1742, *Grosserer-Societetet* (The Merchant Society).

Of the women grocers whose marital status we know, sixteen were married, thirty-eight were widowed, and there was one divorcée. None of the married women's husbands were in the grocery business, so these women were not helping out in a "family economy." Several husbands were in the military, but there were also painters, carpenters, and smiths. Two were "skippers," who might have been ships' captains but could also have just been sailors. In either case, they were probably in the merchant marine and may have brought home goods that their wives then sold.

As for grocers who were widows, about half had inherited their husbands' retail shops on which they continued to pay taxes. These were larger, more established businesses. At least three of these women, all widows—Severine Kreusfelt, Hizilia Meyer, and Johanna Margrethe Schiødt—although listed as grocers (*købmænd*) themselves, nonetheless had had husbands who were wholesalers or merchants. These women paid between one and three portions tax, much more than the other widows. The husbands of the other widows had been in the military or merchant marine, insofar as we know their occupations. The one divorcée, Birgitte Marie Høeg, was given permission "to sell those goods which tea and porcelain dealers are permitted to offer." These were the same goods that her estranged husband also sold.[1]

Purveyors of food also included bakers, butchers, and fishmongers. Although the latter two sold small quantities of meat and fish directly to consumers, bakers were a broader group. Organized in a guild, in 1806 there were fifty-four master guild bakers in the city and 236 journeymen. Yet 102 men and ten women paid taxes as some variety of baker, again proving that many more people were gainfully involved in the trade than were guild members. Titles given for bakers included variations such as bread bakers, cake bakers, French bread bakers, confectioners, and pastry sellers. Guild and other licensed bakers sold their finished baked goods to individuals who then peddled these wares on the streets. Several of these street vendors were discussed in the previous chapter, but Dorothea Müller, the woman who sold to these street vendors, was herself the licensed baker, albeit not a guild member.

Dorothea embodies several elements involved in this research. She had taken over her husband Caspar's license when he died and later passed it on to her son Philip. As the holder of the baker's license herself, she also had the authority to vouch for other women. But piecing together Dorothea's story involves the use of several different records, none of which overlap, so the dates are episodic, some are missing, and her life trajectory is not always clear. The 1787 census already lists Dorothea as a widow, age forty-one, although the date of her husband's death is unknown. Since she is not listed as paying taxes in 1771, Caspar was probably still alive then, meaning that he died sometime between 1771 and 1787. By the time of the 1801 tax records, Dorothea is listed as paying one and one-quarter portion self-employment tax. Fifteen years later, in 1816, she sent the city a list of twenty women who were selling her bread. Using the information from census, tax, and city license records, we can determine that Dorothea ran a successful bakery on her own for at least twenty-nine years, from 1787 until at least 1816.[2] When her son Philip took over is unknown, although he had probably been working with his mother for some time.

Dorothea was one of forty-two women listed as some sort of baker, sixteen of whom paid taxes. The women who paid taxes, anywhere from one-quarter to two portions, were mostly widows, when we know their marital status, whose husbands, when we know their occupations, were mostly bakers themselves. The other twenty-six non-tax-paying women mostly had more specific licenses to sell various kinds of bread, such as rye bread or "French bread" (usually a white or wheat based bread). Of these, only six had husbands who were bakers. Four were widows, one was married, and one divorced. Other husbands were captains, military personnel, journeymen carpenters, and goldsmiths.

None of these sets of numbers are completely coterminous. Whereas the guild records were probably fairly accurate, tax and census figures might reflect the vagaries of time and space; that is, they would depend on who was collecting what information when and for what purpose. They are included to give a sense of scale and proportions. For example, 10 percent of tax-paying bakers were women. Were 10 percent of all bakers women? I suspect that is a minimum and not a maximum number.

The thirty female butchers and fishmongers were a social group similar to the bakers, although the marriages of the butchers seem less stable. Of the twenty-five women butchers, six were divorced, one separated and one presumed abandoned by her husband. This was Marianne Jensen, whose husband was a merchant. She was given permission in 1822 to sell fish and smoked pork for two years, which was later renewed for an additional two years or "until her husband returned."[3] Since Jens Joseph Jensen was a merchant, one might assume that he had gone off on a sailing trip somewhere and never returned. The municipal government was concerned about the ability of his wife to support herself in her husband's absence, but once he returned (*if* he returned), then it was his business to support his wife. The other divorced and separated husbands were all in the meat business. Of the remaining seventeen women butchers, twelve were widows and the other five married. The butchers' guild had sixty-one master butchers in 1805.

There were five women fishmongers, three were widows, one married, and the marital status of one unknown. The two husbands whose occupation is known were both also fishmongers. There was no fishmongers guild. It is important to remember that these were fish *mongers*, not fish*wives*. The former sold from buildings, but the latter from stalls on the streets, by the canals. I assume that the former had more revenue, mostly because their overhead costs, including rent or upkeep on a fixed structure, would have been higher.

The food distribution and service industry also included people who sold or dispensed finished foods for eating or drinking on the premises. In addition to the food sold on the streets, food for immediate consumption was offered in restaurants, inns, bars, dining rooms, and perhaps coffee and tea shops. Restaurants as we know them today, with individual tables and menu choices, probably did not yet exist in Copenhagen. Instead, transients, travelers, and those without their own dining facilities ate at inns or pubs (*værtshuse*) that offered common meals at fixed times. People did not chose what they wanted to eat, nor did they sit at individual tables, but instead ate whatever was served from common platters, family style, at a communal table.[4]

Copenhagen was filled with people who rented rooms, not apartments, and therefore had no place to prepare food. Even apartments often lacked cooking facilities. These people might eat at "boarding" or dining rooms, that is, from hosts who offered food but would not necessarily have a place to sleep (the "board" part of "room and board"). An advertisement in the January 2, 1801, edition of *Adresseavisen*, for example, stated that, "in the second floor corner room at Klosterstræde and Skindergade 39, several respectable people can get dinner at a closed table."[5] The term "closed table" meant that this was a specific and regular group of people who ate together. The "table" was not open to anyone who walked in from the street. The person providing this food was probably a *spisevært*, a "boarding host." A "corner room" probably had windows to two sides, making it a more preferable location.

The wide range of individuals who provided food and drink to residents and transients in Copenhagen functioned under a varied range of titles, although the most common was *værtshusholder*, literally translated as someone who owns an inn or a pub. Also included in this category were caterers, sutlers (civilians who provided food to the military), people running billiard parlors, and club owners. Tea and coffee shop owners are also included here because they provided prepared drinks, although it is not certain that they served food as well. There was also a category of *konditor*, which was either a pastry chef, a confectioner, or the place where such sweets were sold. They are included under bakers, although some of them may also have served their goods for consumption on the spot.[6] That said, at least 112 women had licenses for some sort of food-serving establishment. Of these, thirty paid taxes, anywhere from one-quarter portion to one and one-half portions. About half these tax-paying women were widows, often of men also in the food service business, when we know their occupations. For comparison, 410 men paid taxes in 1801 for some sort of prepared food service. As was the case with women, many more men probably had food licenses than actually paid taxes. This tally, of course, does not include those cooks and chefs who worked in private homes, since they did not need licenses and would not have paid the self-employment tax. It is interesting, however, to pause here and note that whereas only 10 percent of tax-paying butchers were women, women made up one-quarter of tax-paying restauranteurs. This implies that there were many more licensed women on the prepared end of food service than on the raw retail end.

Many of these licenses came with constraints, testifying to governmental interest both in controlling business and in insuring that people (widows mostly) had a source of income. Most common was the stipulation that a widow could retain her license unless or until she remarried. Caroline Andersen, for instance, received a license for "boarding quarters" (i.e., serving prepared meals) in 1820, "so long as she remained a widow." Her husband Hans had been a teamster, so this was a new business for her family.[7] A variant, attesting to a concern for insuring a successful livelihood, was the license issued to Catharina Magdalena Andersen in 1821, also allowing her to maintain "boarding quarters for respectable persons" for two years. Catharina's license came with the stipulation that the license would terminate "if the conditions of the husband's job have improved to such a degree that it is assumed that the wife no longer needs to carry on this business in order to support the family." Her husband worked for the royal lottery and that, according to official authorities, should provide enough income for a family. Since Mr. Andersen probably worked on commission, however, his income would have been unpredictable.[8]

In some cases widows were issued licenses for food service in exchange for returning their husbands' licenses for other occupations. This was true for both Elise Bergeskou and Georgine Berg, who were given permission for tea and coffee shops in 1824 and 1825 respectively. Elise turned in her husband's citizenship papers as a merchant, which would have involved a considerable social decline for Elise but probably left her with something she felt more capable of handling. Georgine renounced her right to continue her husband Christian's occupation as a fishmonger.[9]

Several widows received permission in the 1830s to serve tea and coffee as long as they remained unmarried, paid taxes, and did not allow dancing.[10] Forbidding dancing is an unexpected condition, as we rarely associate dancing with tea or coffee shops today. But elsewhere at the time, in England for example, coffee houses were seen as an antithesis to local taverns or pubs. Coffee was the "great soberer," and coffee houses were places of communication, where serious discussions, often of a political nature, took place.[11] Prohibiting dancing would help to solidify the difference between the places of consumption of these new exotic beverages (coffee and tea) and older establishments where alcohol was served. Since coffee houses were quintessential male space, the dancing prohibition is even more baffling, but women were often present as owners and servers. As coffee houses sprang up across the Copenhagen landscape, they helped to change the nature of the city's geography, as well as its social context and political content.

Another stipulation that frequently showed up on these licenses and is difficult to decode is the restriction that *spiseværter* (hosts, or people who served prepared food) were allowed to serve food and beverages only to people "not of the simple *almue* class." *Almue* is not an easy word to translate. Today's dictionary says it refers to peasants or small farmers. But it is also used to refer to "common folk," or maybe just "folk," in the sense of folk art or folk crafts, which, of course, again refers back to Denmark's peasant traditions. The *Dictionary of the Danish Language* (*Ordbog over det danske sprog*) defines *almue* as "people of lower class and small conditions; little people, especially rural. ... Peasants, servants, artisans, retailers, lower civil servants."[12] Does this mean that these licenses were given to serve only Copenhagen residents, in that *almue*, being mostly rural, would not be residents? But what of servants, artisans, retailers, and civil servants? Was the assumption that they ate elsewhere, with employers or "masters"? Were these establishments to serve exclusively wealthier or poorer customers? One tends to think the latter, people at the very bottom of the social scale, but one wonders if a living could be earned that way. In any case, at least six women were given such licenses in the 1820s—four widowed, one married, one divorced. None of their husbands were in the food industry—three were skippers, one a ropemaker, and one a linen weaver.

One of the largest industries in Copenhagen involved the production and distribution of alcoholic beverages. People in the alcohol trade fell into four distinct categories with very little overlap—*øltappere*, dispensers of beer (in small quantities), *bryggere*, brewers (of beer), *brændeviinsbrændere*, distillers (of hard liquor, mostly *akvavit*), and *vinhandlere*, wine merchants (who would be selling imported goods). Brewers, distillers, and wine merchants were all organized in guilds. Beer dispensers, who had no guild, were the single largest tax-paying occupational category. In the 1801 tax records, five hundred and fifty-six men and women (522 men and 34 women), or 9 percent of the total number of self-employment tax-payers (6,207), paid taxes as beer dispensers. Although there were many of them, beer dispensers individually paid little in taxes, mostly a one-quarter portion, although a handful paid one-half. None paid more than that; this was a small business. Of the fifty-one tax-paying women in this field in 1771 and 1801, 80 percent were widows, and the husbands of half of these widows had also dispensed beer. The occupations of the other husbands are unknown. This was obviously a business that stayed in families. One might assume that wives had helped their husbands while they were still alive. Despite pictures and images of buxom barmaids, only 6.5 percent of tax-paying beer dispensers were women. So there was a higher percentage of women who paid taxes as butchers than as beer dispensers, although there was a greater absolute number of beer dispensers.

Fewer people were engaged in guild-regulated alcohol industries—brewers, distillers, and wine tapsters. Brewers, who were organized in a guild until 1805 when the guild was disbanded, had the highest status among those in the alcohol industry. There were fewer brewers than distillers, only 100 brewers in 1805, and they paid considerably more in taxes than did any of the other groups. The twenty women who paid taxes as brewers paid between one and three portions, although most paid two. Their businesses were large enough that at least two of these women—Elisabeth Christine Berling and Marie Martine Bonfils—will be discussed in the next chapter on business managers. Overwhelmingly, female brewers were widows. Out of the sixty-six whose names are known, forty-one, or 62 percent, were widows, usually of brewers. The marital status of the remaining women is unknown, but they may also have been widows.

The names of many of these women are known because they are listed in a journal kept by municipal secretaries from 1735 to 1805. This was an on-going list of all those employed by the city, starting with The 32 Men of the City Council and continuing on down through the city's "night men" or sanitation workers. Included here was a list, according to an ordinance of 1755, of all journeymen brewers when they swore their oaths as brewers. The list also specified the master brewers who had trained them. Among the "master" brewers were thirty-seven women, although, as women, they could not be and were not guild members. Nonetheless, they obviously had the standing to sponsor journeymen brewers. Seventeen of these women were widows of brewers insofar as we know what their husbands did, but mostly no occupational title was given for husbands.[13]

This offers a good example of the tangled intertwining of women and guilds during this period. Technically not able to be guild members, several women (mostly widows) nonetheless were treated and acted as guild members. Not allowed to vote in guild elections, nor to serve as members of The 32 Men, they nonetheless paid into guild coffers and were able to train and keep journeymen and apprentices. In many cases, this training continued well beyond a husband's death, so it was not just a matter of continuing or finishing up training started by husbands. In addition to Elisabeth Christine Berling, mentioned earlier, at least a dozen other widows sponsored journeymen when they took their oath as brewers. Anna Elisabeth Lorentzen, for instance, who was a widow when she paid two portions self-employment tax in 1771, sponsored six journeymen brewers between 1768 and 1782.

The distillers formed the largest of the alcohol guilds, with 295 master distillers and no journeymen in 1806. Only 265 men paid taxes as distillers in 1801. Nine women paid taxes as distillers; however, there were at least thirty-nine women who had some sort of official contact as distillers. Overwhelmingly, these were widows of distillers. Twenty-four paid taxes in 1771 or 1801. Oddly, the taxes range from one-quarter portion to one and one-half portions; the spread is usually much smaller. Since I have not been able to determine how these taxes were assessed, I cannot begin to venture an explanation. It would seem to prove, however, that taxes were not assessed solely on the basis of occupational title.

In 1742, the city of Copenhagen decided to inspect all 319 distilleries within the city boundaries. The inspectors categorized the distilleries as "proper," "good," or "needing improvement." Those that needed improvement were inspected a second time in a follow-up visit to make sure necessary corrections had been made.[14] Unfortunately for the historian, such an investigation was never done again, or, at least, I have not been able to find one. Of the 319 distillers listed, fourteen were women (4 percent), all widows of distillers.

The wine tapsters guild had sixty-three members in 1806, but there were forty-six people (including one woman) who paid taxes as wine merchants in 1801. I am unsure how much overlap there was between the two groups, but both would have had to deal with imported goods, since Denmark did not have a wine production industry of any sort. Those who wrote against wine as a luxury item differentiated between wine from France (which was seen as particularly "luxurious") and wine from elsewhere, probably from the German states, but in either case, this was an imported item.

At least eight women had permission to act as wine merchants. Four were widows of wine merchants; one was married and in 1741 received a royal privilege to sell wine together with her husband, Friderich Daniel de Pilloy.[15] Taxes paid in 1771 and 1801 ranged anywhere from one-quarter portion to one and one-quarter portions—again, representing quite a large spread within a single occupation. Interestingly, when Philibert Bonfils died in 1773, his oldest son Henrich inherited his license as a wine merchant, while his widow, Marie Martine, continued the Bonfils brewery. Marie Martine's business flourished while Henrich's went bankrupt. This may suggest either that there was more money to be made in brewing or that Henrich was a poor businessman. Supporting the former explanation is the fact that after Henrich died in 1797, and his younger brother Joseph carried on the dealership, Marie Martine continued to pay considerably more in taxes than her son (see next chapter).

Finally, five women (four widows) paid taxes on the production of tobacco in 1801. (I realize that tobacco is neither food nor drink, but since it is a substance that is also imbibed or physically consumed, this seemed a logical place to include it.) One married woman was given a royal privilege in 1756 to sell tobacco, together with her husband, Anders Ørbek. Mrs. Ørbek also received permission to continue with this sale if she should survive her husband.[16] The other women paid taxes on the selling and manufacturing of tobacco; again, taxes ranged from one-quarter (tobacco seller) to one and one-half (tobacco manufacturer). Here the different tax amounts do follow the occupation, tobacco manufacturers paying more than tobacco sellers.

Chart 3.1

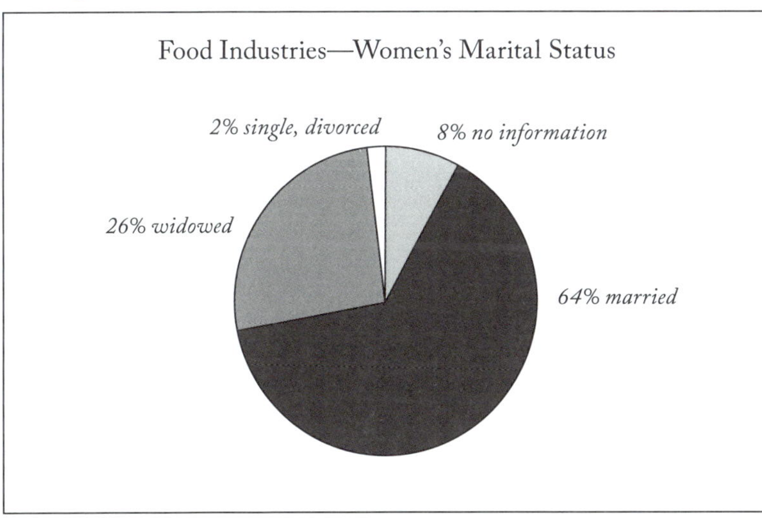

All told, about 46 percent of the women in my database were in the business of producing or distributing food or drink, including tobacco. Of these, 64 percent were married at the time they either received a license or paid taxes. Twenty-six percent were widows, and 2 percent were either single, separated, or divorced. We do not know the marital status of the remaining 8 percent. Of those people who paid self-employment tax in 1801 for work in the food industry, 6 percent were women; however, overall women made up 8 percent of total taxpayers. That means that, despite the perception of food being a quintessential female industry, women were slightly less taxed here than in other industries, although they were heavily involved in it.

Production

Production is a much more diffuse category, involving occupations ranging from milliners through printers and ropemakers to carpenters and bricklayers. In most cases, the person involved was both the producer and the seller. Milliners made women's clothing—and sold it; the same was true of printers, ropemakers, and some carpenters. Laborers such as masons, bricklayers, and transport workers really offered only services, working with materials produced by someone else (bricks or wagons, for example). Even so, we do not really think of construction workers or teamsters as part of the service industry, so I have included them under production. It is a judgment call that could go either way. I have also created a separate category for merchants, non-food shopkeepers, and junk dealers, who were really more involved in distribution than in production. Since they sold, transported, or distributed a variety of goods, they cannot easily be placed in a single productive category.

Certainly, women in the clothing industry come quickly to mind when considering women's occupations. Food and clothing are two of the *acknowledged* occupational categories for women. And indeed they were. The last chapter discussed women who hawked clothing on the streets and in the markets; here the discussion will include those women who *made* the clothing—milliners (who made clothing, not just hats), modistes (who made fashionable clothing for women), and even tailors. Furriers, glovers, hatters, shoemakers, and tailors were all organized in separate guilds. By definition, of course, their membership could not include women, but, as with other occupations, there were women who were nonetheless taxed as practitioners of these occupations.

Table 3.1

Clothing Production

	1806	1801 taxes	
	Guild members (men)	men	women
Furriers	14	10	
Glovers	10	12	
Hatters	23	15	
Shoemakers	410	292	9
Tailors	432	268	6
Milliners		3	1

After beer dispensers, shoemakers were the single largest taxed occupational category in 1801, almost 5 percent of the total. Additionally, a variety of other occupations dealing with clothing were taxed in 1801. Twenty-one men who made stockings, buttons, belts, ribbons, and even corsets all paid some taxes. There was also a variety of weavers, lace and linen makers, calico printers, and fringe makers, again all men. As for the women who produced clothing, in both 1771 and 1801 five paid a small amount of taxes (one-quarter portion) as "tailors," usually understood as producers of men's clothing. They were all widows of tailors. And, in 1804, Anne Hedvig Jansen received permission to "engage in the occupation of tailoring." Her divorced husband, Christian Fredrich Bentzer, was also a tailor.[17]

Most women engaged in some form of clothing production, however, did not pay taxes. It is hard to sort out the varieties of production, but most of those who worked in the field made women's clothing either as milliners or modistes—(*modehandlere*), decorations for women (*damepynt*), or various accessories for women's wardrobes. Just how precise these occupations could be is represented by Elizabeth Weise (or Weys), a "glitterer," who made a living by attaching glitter to fabric. She was a widow and, although listed in the 1801 tax record, paid no taxes that year.[18]

Of the roughly two hundred women who both had permission to carry on some production of women's clothes or accessories and whose marital status we know, slightly over half were widows (53 percent), 30 percent were married, 12 percent were single, and 5 percent were divorced. Non-tax-paying widows' husbands had only very rarely been tailors themselves, although several were shoemakers. Occupations of other deceased husbands had ranged widely—ship's captain, painter, wine merchant, weaver, various military titles, even one judge. A similar spread is true for husbands who were still alive. Even husbands who were divorced, with the exception of Christian Fredrich Bentzer, were not tailors; they included a dentist, a hatter, a miller, and three shoemakers. Divorcées were often given permission to carry on their husbands' businesses as long as they remained unmarried. A similar proviso was attached to licenses given to single women.

As was true of women who hawked clothing products on the streets, women who worked with clothing products from within fixed structures rarely made a lot of money. But even if they did not pay taxes, and most of them did not, government authorities believed that such occupations provided enough support for a woman who was on her own. Of course, government "poverty levels" were notoriously low, but her work probably produced enough income to keep her off the poor rolls.

Many other women were engaged in production industries less often associated with their gender. For instance, at least sixteen women, all widows, were publishers, printers, or booksellers. This trade seemed to run in families, and many of the women in the book business were daughters or widows of printers, or publishers. In the late eighteenth century, between fourteen and twenty presses were functioning in Copenhagen. Although Harold Ilsøe does not have separate entries for women in his 1992 study, *Bogtrykkerne i København* (Printers in Copenhagen), he does list fifteen women in his index, all widows; ten dated from the eighteenth century.[19] (See the discussion of Elisabeth Christine Berling in the next chapter for a particularly successful printing family.) Dorothe Morthorst, for example, took over her husband Johan Frederik's printing business and ran it with her son-in-law, Carl Dahlén. Dahlén was also a dancer and inspector at the Royal Theater. In 1798, they took over the press at Adressekontoret, which printed *Adresseavisen,* a Copenhagen paper with classified advertisements and official notices. Dorothe paid one portion in self-employment tax in 1801, so the business clearly continued to be successful.[20] Most women paid considerably less in taxes, usually one-quarter or one-half portion.

Even less obviously engaged in "women's" business were the sixty women who paid taxes for professions in the building trades and as various kinds of metal smiths. These women were all widows, and all inherited their husbands' businesses. Nonetheless, they were conducting business in their own names as carpenters (11), glaziers (4), masons and bricklayers (4), roofers (3), and painters (2). Women also participated in various metal trades as smiths, working with gold, brass, pewter, iron, and copper. Among other products, they made and sold swords and guns. Elisabeth Buck, for example, was given permission in 1831 to continue her husband's business as a goldsmith after his death.[21] After her husband's death left her alone with two small daughters in 1801, Anne Margrethe Walström received permission to carry on her husband's business as a coppersmith and to maintain a journeyman.[22]

Women engaged in other forms of production were also mostly widows, to the extent we know their marital status. Birgithe Morthorst, however, was allowed by the Ropemakers Guild to continue to function as a "master," because her husband had disappeared, leaving her with three small children. In 1787, she was living on Gothersgade with her children and two lodgers, a skipper and his wife. By 1801, fourteen years later, she had moved to Christianshavn, in a neighborhood that was not as good as her previous apartment, and was living with her youngest son, Hans Jørgen, as lodgers in the household of Christen Sørensen, a day watchman. This represents a definite social decline. Birgithe's daughter, Johanne Kirstine, however, did better. At age twenty, she was married to Jacob Bierregaard, who was forty years old, a master ropemaker, and they lived at Nyhavn 55, in a three-story house that Jacob owned.[23] Nyhavn would be a particularly useful address for a ropemaker, since ships lined the canal (*Nyhavn* means "new harbor"), and ships were probably Bierregaard's chief market.

Another woman ropemaker, Karen Mariager, also provides a good example of the pattern of people staying within familial trades. Karen received a license in 1793 to continue her late husband Christian's trade as ropemaker and to travel to markets on Sjælland selling the rope she made. Her father, Niels, had also been a ropemaker, who paid one-quarter portion tax in 1771, as did Karen in 1801, so Karen had married within the family trade. She also, apparently, received permission to continue to maintain and train apprentices within the rope trade, because on October 27, 1801, her apprentice H. Bentzen filed a complaint with the police that he had been "let go." Since this was at least eight years after Christian's death, Bentzen would seem to have been a new apprentice and not one of Christian's. Intriguingly, a week later, Karen reported a break-in and property theft to the police. One cannot help wondering if Bentzen were somehow involved.[24]

Seven women paid taxes as candlemakers. All of them were widows of candlemakers, so this is obviously a continuation of their husbands' businesses. There was also a handful of women who produced sails, saddles, wagons, clocks, carpets, cards, and bottle corks; two women ran soap "factories." Other women were just listed in tax records as owning "factories." (See the next chapter for a discussion of two women who ran very successful "factories"—Frederica Louise Ernst, who had a linseed oil factory, and Else Fenger, who ran a soap factory.)

Nine women, all widows, paid taxes on some sort of business providing transportation for hire. Karen Sophia Nörager was given a royal privilege in 1769 for three street wagons, one coach, and one "chaise" (an open two-horse, two-person vehicle), in order to support her four small children after her husband died. The license was for use in Copenhagen and was meant for her children to inherit when they were old enough to earn their own livings.[25] In 1804, Cecilia Anne Cathrine Toldberg, a divorcée, was given a license to offer transport for hire, as had her divorced husband, Søren Andersen Toldberg.[26]

The practice of allowing divorced women to continue in the business of their estranged husbands raises a couple of interesting points. Obviously, the government's interest was in enabling women to care for themselves so that they should not become a burden on society, but it also presupposes that these women had the knowledge and capability to carry on in these professions. In this, municipal and royal authorities often ran counter to guild interests. Guilds tried to maintain both the "mystery" and mastery of the craft in question, as well as to limit the number of master craftsmen so as to limit the competition. Deborah Simonton has written of guilds that "[a]pprenticeship was one mechanism for controlling women in society and for protecting male preserves and 'maleness'."[27] Allowing divorced women to continue in the profession ran counter to all those interests. Late eighteenth-century Danish governmental authorities used the situation of divorced women as a mechanism to chip away at guild monopolies,

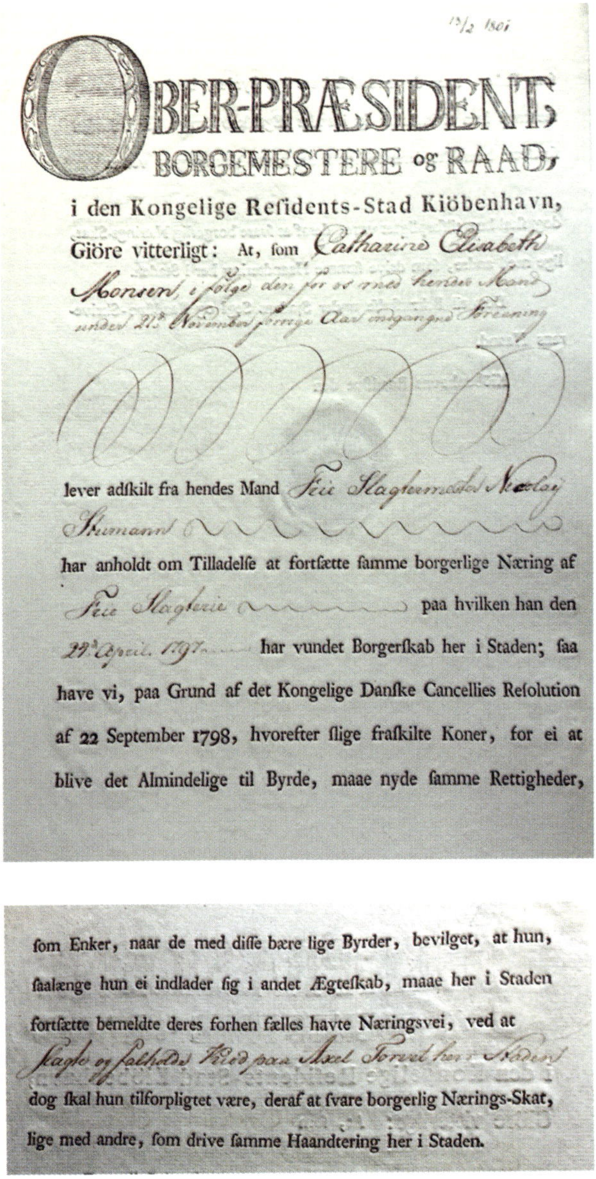

13/2 1801

OBER-PRÆSIDENT, BORGEMESTERE og RAAD, i den Kongelige Reſidents-Stad Kiöbenhavn, Giöre vitterligt: At, ſom Catharine Elisabeth Monsen, i følge den for os med hendes Mand under 21de November forrige Aar indgangne Forening

lever adſkilt fra hendes Mand Fiie Slagtermester Nicolay Stumann

har anholdt om Tilladelſe at fortſætte ſamme borgerlige Næring af Fiie Slagterie paa hvilken han den 29de April 1797 har vundet Borgerſkab her i Staden; ſaa have vi, paa Grund af det Kongelige Danſke Cancellies Reſolution af 22 September 1798, hvorefter ſlige fraſkilte Koner, for ei at blive det Almindelige til Byrde, maae nyde ſamme Rettigheder,

ſom Enker, naar de med diſſe bære lige Byrder, bevilget, at hun, ſaalænge hun ei indlader ſig i andet Ægteſkab, maae her i Staden fortſætte bemeldte deres forhen fælles havte Næringsvei, ved at ſlagte og falholde Kiød paa Axel Torvet her i Staden; dog ſkal hun tilforpligtet være, deraf at ſvare borgerlig Nærings-Skat, lige med andre, ſom drive ſamme Haandtering her i Staden.

Fig. 3.1. Christiane Elisabeth Monsen's butcher license. Københavns Raadstue, "Betieninger," Copenhagen City Archives.[28]

not because they had any feminist or proto-feminist beliefs, but simply to lessen guild influence and to support citizens who might otherwise have a claim on government support. Indeed, there were apparently so many licenses issued to divorced women that the municipal government had pre-printed forms for these cases. Figure 3.1 is a copy of the license issued to Catharine Elisabeth Monsen to continue in her husband's business as a butcher. Part of the preprinted form states that she "lives separated from her husband."

There is space left in the printed form to write in the woman's name, her husband's name, his occupation, and the date he received "citizenship" for his occupation. The form is also quite clear that the woman named, "so as not to be a burden to the public, shall have the same rights as widows."

Service Industries

Since preindustrial Copenhagen was largely a service center for the government, military, and merchant marine, it should come as no surprise to find a large number of people engaged in service industries, among whom were midwives, educators, and civil servants. Unquestionably, the single largest group in this category were midwives. There were at least five hundred women who were licensed as midwives in Copenhagen between 1719 and 1819. By definition, midwives were women, and, by custom, they were supposed to have given birth to at least one child, which further meant an assumption that they were or had been married. Gordon Norrie found only two unmarried midwives in Copenhagen in the eighteenth century, but both were engaged and about to be married.[29] According to an ordinance of November 30, 1714, midwives had to be "examined and taught" by the Midwife Commission, consisting of medical faculty from the university. They were also to spend time in a hands-on practicum with practicing midwives, so that they could better understand that which they had studied theoretically. Not until paragraph 5 did the ordinance state that midwives were to show "a godly and respectable attitude … and be well learned in Christendom." They were also to stay on good terms with each other, so that they could help out in emergencies. Midwives were to serve the poor as well as the rich and not engage in any medical cures, except in acute emergencies, and even then using only medication readily available at apothecaries.

Fig. 3.2
Katrine Marie Poulsen's midwife sign, 1785,
Danish National Museum, Copenhagen.

Midwives were absolutely prohibited from providing women with any form of abortifacient. According to Norrie, this ordinance remained the basis for midwifery in Copenhagen for the next two hundred years.[30]

The city kept records of midwives, who are listed in several places, including lists of "citizens," of people who received business licenses, and of all those who were "employed" by the city of Copenhagen. "Employment" is a flexible term here and does not mean that the people so listed were actually salaried by the city, but rather that they served in some official capacity, since it also included, for example, the members of the City Council and the heads of the guilds.[31]

The number of midwives in Copenhagen was set at thirty in 1714 and expanded to sixty in 1743. This cap was, however, eliminated by a 1797 ordinance that stated that "every midwife examined and found capable may have permission, immediately after successfully passing the exam, to hang out a sign in Copenhagen."[32] In a few cases, daughters succeeded their mothers in this business, as was the case with the two unmarried women, but more frequently the successor to the license was someone else entirely. Husbands, when we know what they did, which is not often, belonged to the same petit bourgeois background as the other husbands with whom we have been dealing in this chapter. There were several journeymen, a small handful of master craftsmen, and members of the military, both army and navy.

In terms of other medical services, there were five women barbers (who could also be surgeons)[33] and one apothecary. All six were widows. Barbers were organized in a guild, which in 1805 had twenty master barbers. Anne Cathrine Schule applied in 1802 for permission "to carry on in the profession of barber and to keep a journeyman." She was granted this permission. Anne Cathrine's husband, Balthasser, had been a musketeer, so this was not a common situation, but perhaps she had acted as a barber before she was widowed.[34] Of the other husbands, there was a barber, a district surgeon, and an apothecary. One woman, Dine Bente Solle, had a son who was also a district surgeon. So, excluding the musketeer, most of these women remained within the medical business of the family.

In the eighteenth and very early nineteenth centuries, there were approximately 250 women who owned and ran private proprietary schools for girls. Although the law introducing compulsory education in Denmark dates from 1814, there had been female schoolkeepers in Copenhagen dating back to the seventeenth century.[35] Despite the stereotype of these women as illiterate spinsters, they all could read, and the overwhelming majority could write as well, as shown by the fact that the great majority wrote their own application letters, and all of the women signed their own names. Additionally, after the introduction of the 1814 School Law, applicants could be asked to prove their literacy through a so-called "paragraph 58 test." Members of the Copenhagen School Board dutifully noted when a woman could not write and usually refused a license on this ground.[36] It should be remembered that Denmark was a Lutheran country by this time, and people therefore had to pass literacy tests in order to be confirmed. Since confirmation was necessary in order to be considered a "civil person" who had reached one's majority, most Danes of the time could read, if not necessarily write. For the preponderance of Danes, who were Lutheran, the ability to read Luther's *Small Catechism* was proof of literacy. The small percentage of Danes who were Jewish, Catholic, or non-Lutheran Protestants had to pass similar literacy tests in order to be accorded "civil" status.

Of the 76 percent of the female schoolkeepers whose marital status we know, 40 percent were married, 33 percent widowed, and 27 percent single. These figures vary from others in terms of marital status, particularly in the large number of single women. We also have information about a higher percentage of husbands, or their absence. I think the reason is that these women tended to write their life stories when applying for business licenses. Several of these women were members of "teaching families," where husbands and sometimes sons or sons-in-law were also in the business. One such example was Elise Engelsen, who opened a girls school in 1789, the year she married Hans Engelsen. Elise was thirty-three at the time. Hans had originally been a carpenter but had opened his own boys school in 1773. When Hans died in 1803, his school was taken over by Johan Jacob, Hans's son by his first wife. Johan Jacob died seven years later, in 1810, and the school continued under the ownership and management of a young teacher, Odin Tidemand, age twenty. Four years later, Tidemand married Johan Jacob's widow. Elise continued to run her own school at the same address as Tidemand ran her late husband's school. The two schools shared many of the same teachers. So here we have two schools, side by side, run by a female schoolkeeper and her step-daughter-in-law's second husband.[37]

Husbands and fathers who were schoolkeepers, school teachers, principals, clergymen, and deacons, all of whom could be said to be in the business of education, made up the largest category of male relatives of women schoolkeepers. The next largest category of male relatives consisted of those involved in some fashion in the navy or merchant marine. In other words, these were husbands who were probably absent from home for long periods of time, leaving wives to fend for themselves and their families. Typically, men in the merchant marine did not get paid while at sea, but rather received a lump sum "crew share" when the ship returned to its home port. Considering the length of some voyages, families could have difficulty making ends meet during husbands' absences.[38] Other husbands were craftsmen and artisans, both masters and journeymen. Although Birthe Christine Ernst's husband "lived a disordered life," most husbands seem to have been responsible members of the middle and lower middle classes.[39]

Rounding out women in the service industries were a small number of women civil servants. Although this sounds like an oxymoron, there were, nonetheless, some circumstances in which a woman's expertise was necessary. At the beginning of life, with childbirth, obviously a woman was necessary, but also at the end of life. Women were hired to assess the value of another woman's property when she died. Such a woman was called an "assessment woman" (*vurderingskone*), and the city hired a small number of them. I know of six, although I believe that there were to be three available at any given time. The six whose names I know were all licensed in mid-century (1751–66) and are listed in the record book of city personages. There must have been others who simply were not listed. Of these six, three were widowed, one married, and the marital status of the other two is not given.

There were also a handful of auctioneers (six), half of whom were widows of auctioneers. I know their names because they all paid between one-quarter and one-half portion taxes in 1771 and 1801. There were probably others.

The women discussed in this chapter made up the bulk of the independent working women in preindustrial Copenhagen. As 8 percent of self-employment tax-payers, they were inextricably woven throughout the city's preindustrial urban economy. They were so ubiquitous that no one thought to mention it at the time, any more than one would single out or draw attention to the existence of male workers. It is only now, looking back through the prism of nineteenth-century domestic ideology, that their presence is consciously noted and acknowledged. Additionally, as we have seen in this chapter, women were engaged in the entire gamut of occupations, not just in the food and service industries where "common wisdom" expects to find them. Women were bricklayers, carpenters, smiths (including sword makers), barbers, and civil servants. The only places one did *not* find women were in the clergy, the military, and as members of the municipal government.

Various legal and social loopholes both allowed and encouraged women to become and remain active in the economy of the period. Although technically needing their husbands' permission to act in the work force, the social mores of the time accepted independent working women, thus allowing them considerable freedom within legal parameters. The fact that a man had to actively deny his wife the right to work must have fostered an assumption on the part of young girls and women that they would be able to work on their own. Additionally, the legal right of a widow to retain control of her husband's business must have meant that young girls grew up with the knowledge and assumption that they too could inherit the family property and business. After all, daughters would have seen mothers taking over and continuing to manage family businesses.

The fact that widows continued to work in guild trades, despite the prohibition on women in guilds, must have further impressed young girls about their future possibilities. The royal government's continued pressure on guild privileges helped to create additional possibilities for women. By allowing widows and divorcées to remain in their husbands' occupations, the government was chipping away at guild prerogatives. This created a loophole through which women could, and did, maneuver, further increasing their participation in the urban labor market.

It is quite evident that women did make use of all of the possibilities for working and carrying on business. No apparent barriers existed to women entering into contracts, borrowing money, retaining and training journeymen, or any of the other legal requirements of a successful business. Olwen Hufton has referred to an "economy of expedients," a term she uses "to imply reliance on a multiplicity of small income sources."[40] Women made do. But I would suggest that women more than just "made do." They were active participants in their own lives and made wide-ranging use of all the varied opportunities available to them.

Chapter Four

In the Corner Office: Women Business Managers

Preindustrial Copenhagen was a flourishing, thriving city. Its merchant marine brought in needed goods that were then distributed throughout the city and the country. Foodstuffs were grown outside the city and brought into town for sale. The city also processed sugar, textiles, and other commodities that were then sold for local and national use. Throughout this entire process, women were present. They worked, produced, sold, and managed necessary products for the city's consumption and use. They functioned openly and legally in the urban economy. Many may also have functioned within a grey or shadow economy, where they are harder to trace, but a sizable number of women worked within the legal economy. They made use of customs and laws to control their own narratives. Times may have been hard, but life went on and women contributed to this process.

Alongside the women who worked at the lower end of the economy, selling on the streets and in the markets, and the women who worked in solid brick and timber structures, there was another small group of women who functioned at the upper end of the socio-economic scale. Occupying large mansions, often with separate summer estates, these women often worked alongside, and may even have employed, their poorer sisters. Although all the women in this book owned their own businesses, there was a small group whose businesses were considerably larger. We may call them "business managers" or perhaps "entrepreneurs."

A substantial distance existed between the woman who sold bread on the streets and the woman who ran her own publishing house or soap factory. It had to do with scale, the size of the business. But how is size to be determined? By gross income, or by the number of employees? Both of these would be good measures, if we had the relevant information, but we often do not. Income and bottom line figures are hidden somewhere in the mist of lost records. Census records could possibly reveal the number of employees, but only insofar as apprentices and journeymen were living in the owner's household. In the newer factory and joint stock company arrangements, employees did not live with employers. Nor would the existence of one or two apprentices or journeymen in a household be enough to define a business manager. Gundel Maria Munk, a drysalter who traveled the country selling hemp and dried fish at markets, had a journeyman named Tobias Ritzow as a member of her household for over fifteen years, yet one would not label Gundel Maria a "business manager."

Instead, I have used self-employment tax payments as an indication of business size. According to tax records from 1771 and 1801, approximately 6,000 people in any given year paid this tax. In both years, approximately 7 percent of these tax-payers were women. Taxes were levied in "portions" or in fractions of portions. First, a total tax amount was determined for the entire city. This figure was then divided into 2,000 portions or fractions thereof. Although a few men paid as much as six portions in tax, most women, or their companies, paid three portions or less. In 1771, there were three women who each paid three portions tax: Elisabeth Christine Berling, brewer and publisher; Madame Halkiær, brewer; and Catarina Gustmeyer, merchant. Thirty years later, three and one-half portions were levied on C.S. Black's Widow & Co. This was the most tax that any woman paid, and it was levied not on the Widow Black herself but on the firm as a landlord and merchant, although Johanne (who was C.S. Black's widow) had died the previous year. Three other women each paid three portions tax in 1801: Elisabeth Christine Berling; Hizilia Meyer, merchant, and Marthe Noe, brewer. All three were widows.[1]

Table 4.1

Top Women Self-Employment Tax-Payers

Portions	1771	1801
3½		1 merchant
3	2 brewers 1 merchant	2 brewers 1 retailer
2½	1 merchant 1 gold thread worker	
2	8 brewers 1 trader 4 unknown	8 brewers 2 merchants 1 each innkeeper landlord retailer miller dressmaker
Total	18	19

If we include all women who paid two portions and up, there were still only eighteen (1771) or nineteen (1801) women—or approximately 8 percent of tax-paying women. Just over half of the women who paid the most in taxes were brewers—twenty out of a total of thirty-seven—split evenly over these thirty years. The next highest occupational concentration of tax-payers were merchants, perhaps including one "trader"—six out of thirty-seven, or 16 percent. "Merchants" were wholesalers, who often engaged in shipping as well; retailers had only a single small shop.

For comparison's sake, in 1771, of the 215 women who paid this tax, 168 (78 percent) paid less than one full portion. Indeed, twenty-eight are listed as paying no tax at all, although their names are included. Perhaps they had paid tax at some earlier point, or perhaps their husbands had paid taxes. For whatever reason, their names were carried forward. The percentages are similar thirty years later, in 1801. Of the 240 women who paid this tax in 1801, 183 (76 percent) paid less than one portion tax, of whom twenty-four paid no tax at all.[2]

Women at the lower end of the taxed scale included distillers (of hard liquor, as opposed to brewers of beer, who made much more money),

Chart 4.1

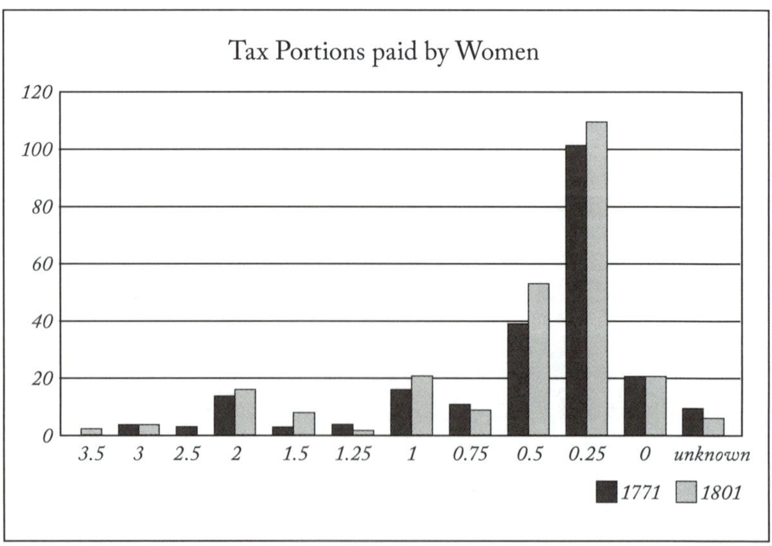

beer dispensers (who sold beer in small quantities), various kinds of retail grocers and dressmakers, innkeepers of several sorts, and even one wagonmaker. (See appendix 3.1 for a listing of all tax-paying occupational titles.) But none of these women were really "business managers." If we concentrate on those women who paid the most in taxes, then we will be dealing primarily with brewers and merchants.

The biggest caveat is available information. My material all comes from official documents—tax records, census forms, applications for various business licenses, guild accounts, and probate records. This means that material about a person emerges at a point of contact with the government, and rarely anywhere else. These were all "well-behaved" women who obeyed the laws and regulations, and, as we know, such women seldom leave records. Hence, the focus here is on a handful of women, about whom some information has managed to survive—and be accessible—two hundred years later. Even with these women, though, we rarely know the entire story. Information has had to be pieced together from multiple sources, but this often still leaves gaping holes in their stories. What follows, then, are admittedly incomplete pictures, but together they may begin to give a sense of this group of women.

These women, while far from representative, nonetheless all represent the *possible.* It was possible for women at the time to control their own businesses—to buy, sell, enter into contracts, train apprentices, and keep journeymen. Although they could not be formal guild members, they often participated in guild businesses. Women were also members of *Grosserer-Societetet* (The Merchants Society).

Table 4.2

Examples of Women as Business Managers

Examples of Women as Business Managers
Elisabeth Christine Berling (1744–1801), brewer and publisher
Marie Martine Bonfils (1731–1804), brewer
Johanne Wadum Black Erichsen (1747–1800), merchant
Catarina Gustmeyer (1710–1773), ship owner and timber merchant
Frederica Louise Ernst (1714–1781), factory owner and West Indian agent
Else Brock Fenger (1737–1811), soap factory owner
Anette Lucie Benedicte Linde (1763–1815), schoolkeeper

The above-mentioned women, with the exception of Ernst (who never married) and Linde (who was married when she started her business), were all widowed and took over their deceased husbands' businesses. The Danish law that allowed widows to continue in husbands' unprobated estates made it legally easy and relatively common for widows to do so. This practice allowed a widow the full use of the estate unless she remarried, a situation of which many widows availed themselves. Of these widows, only Johanne Wadum remarried.

Elisabeth Christine Berling—brewer and publisher

In 1772, Elisabeth Christine Godiche married Georg Christopher Berling. Georg Christopher was the second son of Ernst Henrich Berling, a German printer who had immigrated to Denmark in 1731 and became the Berling family patriarch. Ernst Henrich quickly established himself in the printing industry and married Cecile Høpfner, the daughter of the printer for whom he worked. He opened his own business in 1749 and started an independent periodical, *Berlingske Tidende* (The Berling Times), which still exists today.[3] He received a royal printing and franking privilege for the paper.[4]

Denmark had something very close to freedom of the press in the late eighteenth century. As early as 1755, King Frederik V had urged public debate of "all matters which can increase the prosperity of the country," and, in 1770, a cabinet order simply abolished the royal censor as "harmful to the impartial investigation of the truth." This action was followed a year later with the stipulation that an author's or publisher's name must be included on everything printed, but a prepublication censor was never reintroduced. Publications flourished, and about twenty presses were operating in late eighteenth-century Copenhagen. But the Berlings' royal privilege was unique.[5]

Both the Berling parents died in 1750, and the printing business was continued by their two oldest sons, Johan Christian (born 1733) and Georg Christopher (born 1737). Teenagers (aged seventeen and thirteen), they were under the guardianship of Ludolph Henrich Lillie until 1755, when Lillie left to open his own press. The Berling brothers, now on their own, expanded the business and in 1764 bought a building on Pilestræde, where the press continued until very recently and still has offices.

The property (*gaard*) contained several structures around a courtyard,

Fig. 4.1. Silhouette of Elisabeth Christine Berling. The Museum of Danish National History, Frederiksborg Castle.

including a brewery, with a built-in brewing vat. Deciding to continue with the brewery, Georg Christopher took out citizenship papers (*borgerbrev*) as a brewer in 1765. Brewers were organized in a guild until 1805, when the guild disbanded. Under guild regulations, the number of master brewers in the city was capped at 100, which of course included no women. Nevertheless, in 1801, eighty-nine men and eleven women paid taxes as brewers.[6] One wonders what, if any, training Georg Christopher had as a brewer. In 1802, thirty-seven years after he had started in the brewing business, he did finally receive permission to join the guild.[7]

Both brothers moved in to reside as well as work in the building on Pilestræde, albeit in separate apartments. They decided to split the business so that Johan Christian ran the press and Georg Christopher the brewery. It should be noted that breweries had much higher status at the time and generally paid considerably more in taxes, so it would appear that Georg Christopher got the more profitable side of the business, while his older brother continued in the "family" trade.

Fig. 4.2. Postcard with the Berling brothers and their building, celebrating 200 years in Pilestræde. Georg Christopher is the silhouette on the right.
The Danish Royal Library, Copenhagen.

The brothers soon married, perhaps because they were now well established. In 1766, Georg Christopher married Maria Catharina Godiche, a cousin on his mother's side, also from a printing family. Johan Christian married Anna Marie Frick the following year. The marriages did not last long, cut short by deaths. Johan Christian died in 1771, two months before the birth of his only child, also named Johan Christian. Maria Catharina, Georg Christopher's wife, after giving birth to four stillborn children, died in childbirth with the fifth, in 1772. Six months later the widower married his wife's younger sister, Elisabeth Christine. The couple had two sons, Ernst Andreas (born 1774) and Carl Christian (born 1776), before Georg Christopher died in 1778.[8]

Thus, by 1778, the Berling family consisted of two sisters-in-law (aged thirty-seven and thirty-three), both widowed, and three young male cousins, aged seven, four, and two. Elisabeth Christine was allowed to retain her husband's property, unprobated, "as long as she remains a widow."[9] By this time, the brewery and the publishing house had been combined, since Georg Christopher inherited the publishing business when his older brother died. Anna Marie (Johan Christian's widow) was apparently not interested in running either business, so Elisabeth Christine took over management of both the brewery and the publishing house. There is an extant lawyers' bill from 1788, written out to "Madame Berling," for a Supreme Court case against University Publisher Johan Friderick Schultz. Schultz had apparently tried to move into the publishing of political documents, which had been the prerogative of the Berling press. Schultz lost the case, and the Berling press was confirmed in its monopoly. Elisabeth Christine must have acquiesced in, if not authorized, the suit, which shows some considerable level of involvement in the press's activities. The lawyers charged 261 *rigsdaler*, 5 *skilling*, a sizable sum, attesting to the importance of the Berling monopoly.[10]

Elisabeth Christine also inherited the Godiche family press, *Godicheske Bogtrykkeri,* from her mother, Anna Magdelena Høpfner Godiche, when the latter died in 1789. Anna Magdelena, who also came from a publishing family, had inherited the press from her husband in 1769 and had run it for eleven years, providing evidence of another successful businesswoman. When advertising books for sale from her mother's press, Elisabeth Christine signed herself "E. Christ. Godiche, sal. [widow] Berlings." Advertisements for books published and sold by the Berling press, however, listed "Mad. E. C. Berling in Pilestræde nr. 93" as the source for books.[11] Both wordings made it quite clear that Elisabeth Christine was the responsible party under the terms of the 1771 edict.

Elisabeth Christine Godiche, whose father was a printer and whose mother had successfully continued the business she had inherited as a widow, most certainly knew the printing business when she married Georg Christopher Berling in 1772. Both families—the Godiches and the Berlings—were printers, even Georg Christopher's mother, who was also a Høpfner, came from a printing family. These families intermarried and socialized together. One can assume that these women were conversant with the family business, as evidenced by their continuing success after inheriting the presses.

During Elisabeth Christine's tenure as publisher, *Berlingske Tidende* became the newspaper of record for official public announcements. It started with probate announcements, which had previously been delivered orally in court. *Berlingske Tidende* started printing these notices. They then gradually began printing other official announcements, a segment of the market on which they managed to obtain and maintain a monopoly. This added, of course, to their subscription list and readership. Vogel-Jørgensen, who wrote a bicentennial account of the Berling publishing house in 1949, gives Elisabeth Christine no credit whatsoever for this change. He does, however, admit that "it is hardly an exaggeration to say that, with time, this provision became the cornerstone of the Berling privilege."[12]

The other important trend during Elisabeth Christine's lifetime was the expansion of *Lærde Efterretninger* (The Learned News), which was published by the Berling Press, as one of the leading critical literary magazines of the period. Vogel-Jørgensen, who grudgingly gives both widows (Elisabeth Christine and Anna Marie) credit for this development, says that *Lærde Efterretninger*, together with Knud Rahbek's *Minerva*, were the two most important literary journals of the period.[13] There is no reason to assume that Elisabeth Christine, at least, was not aware of and involved in these changes, even if she herself was not the editor of either the newspaper or the journal. She was the publisher and, under law, the legally responsible person.

But if Elisabeth was running the publishing and printing businesses, who was running the brewery? Apparently, Elisabeth was doing that as well, as a number of documents give her name in that connection. The record of Copenhagen's "citizens" (*Borgerskab Protokol*) lists several apprentices who took oaths as journeymen with Elisabeth Berling over a number of years, so she was obviously deemed capable of overseeing the training of journeymen brewers. A less positive occurrence took place in 1780, when a journeyman coppersmith was sent out to check on the Berling brewing vat. He was not happy with its condition and asked the head of the Brewers Guild to check. He, in turn, sent two master coppersmiths out. They reported back that Madame Berling was present during their inspection and that the vat had "ten to twelve inches of muck" in its bottom. There is no further information, so the resolution of the "muck problem" is unknown. What is clear is that Madame Berling carried enough weight to be intimidating to the coppersmiths sent to check on her.[14]

The Copenhagen city police also received complaints against Madame Berling. Deliveryman Peter Wellau filed a grievance in 1801 against "Mad. Berling's people" (a journeyman and a "boy") for not delivering beer that had been ordered. In 1802, Anders Jørgensen, one of her journeymen, complained to the Brewery Commission that the Berlings were selling watered-down beer. The Commission ruled that this beer should indeed be sold at lower prices, but it also fined the complainant, Anders Jørgensen, two *rigsdaler* for court costs. By then, though, Elisabeth Christine had already died.[15]

Elisabeth Christine Berling died on December 9, 1801. Her obituary was one of the first ones printed in *Berlingske Tidende* as an obituary of a person, rather than as a notice of a change in the condition of a business. Management of the Berling businesses was then taken over by the three cousins—now aged thirty, twenty-seven, and twenty-four—who continued the firm with their fathers' name, "The Brothers Berling." Neither of the two elder cousins, Johan Christian and Ernst Andreas Hartvig, married, so the Berling printing company eventually continued under the auspices of the descendants of the youngest cousin, Carl Christian. The brewery, which was run by Hartvig (Ernst Andreas Hartvig), continued until 1821, nine years after Hartvig's death. Presumably one of the other cousins continued the brewery during that time, but after that it seems to disappear from the saga.[16]

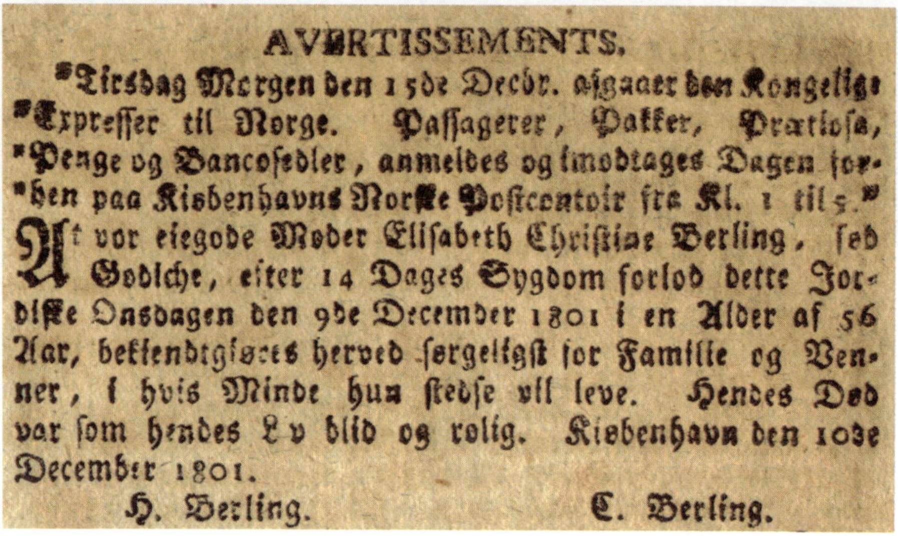

AVERTISSEMENTS.

"Tirsdag Morgen den 15de Decbr. afgaaer den Kongelige "Expresser til Norge. Passagerer, Pakker, Pratiosa, "Penge og Bancosedler, anmeldes og imodtages Dagen for- "hen paa Kiøbenhavns Norske Postcontoir fra Kl. 1 til 5."

At vor eiegode Moder Elisabeth Christine Berling, fød Godiche, efter 14 Dages Sygdom forlod dette Jordiske Onsdagen den 9de December 1801 i en Alder af 56 Aar, bekiendtgiøres herved sørgeligst for Familie og Venner, i hvis Minde hun stedse vil leve. Hendes Død var som hendes Liv blid og rolig. Kiøbenhavn den 10de December 1801.

H. Berling. C. Berling.

Fig. 4.3. Elisabeth Christine Berling's obituary, starting on the fifth line, *Berlingske Tidender*, Dec. 11, 1801.

That our kind hearted mother, Elisabeth Christine Berling, née Godiche, after 14 days illness, left this earth Wednesday, the 9th of December, 1801, at an age of 56 years, we sadly make known to family and friends, in whose memory she will always live. Her death was, like her life, kind and peaceful. Copenhagen, the 10th of December, 1801.

H. Berling C. Berling

For twenty-three years, then, the Berling "empire" was led by women, presumably Elisabeth Christine (longer, if we include the period from 1769 to 1780 when Anna Magdelena Høpfner Godiche ran the press she had inherited from her husband and then passed on to her daughter, Elisabeth Christine). Throughout this period, it retained its royal printing and franking privileges, expanded, and flourished. The brewery, which the Berling brothers had bought in 1764 from Jens Rasmussen, was paying two portions in self-employment tax at the time. From 1766 until at least 1806, the press and the brewery, under the name of "the Berling heirs," regularly paid three portions tax. In 1811, the Berling heirs paid five portions, a very high amount (the highest amount paid was six portions, and very few paid this much).[17]

There is an unusual amount of information available about the Berling family, partly because the family and the newspaper they printed continue to exist and partly because, as printers, they left extant printed records. It is, still, a custom in Denmark to write songs and poems to mark family events—births, marriages, anniversaries, deaths. A collection of these, printed by the Berlings for Berling family events from 1750 to 1808 and bound together in two volumes, is available at the Royal Library in Copenhagen. The family genealogy has been pieced together from these songs (see genealogy in Appendix 4.1).[18]

According to a list put out by the Copenhagen Police Department in December 1806, there were fifty-four master bookbinders in the city, with 236 journeymen and fourteen apprentices. Since these were all guild members, no women were included, as women could not legally be guild members. Nonetheless, earlier, in 1801, twenty-eight men and four women had paid taxes as bookbinders. Printers did not have a guild, so they were not included in this list, but fourteen men and five women paid taxes as printers. Additionally, fifteen men (no women) paid taxes as booksellers. There is undoubtedly much occupational overlap here; printers, for example, often also sold books. We know, for example, that Elisabeth Christine did. She is not, however, included here; her occupation is listed simply as "brewer" in the tax records, although the 1801 city directory gives her title as "brewer- and printer-widow."[19]

Elisabeth Christine Berling was thus not the only woman printer. During the 1700s, there were at least nine female printers in Copenhagen at one time or another, all widows who inherited their husbands' businesses, of whom several later married other printers. In these cases, it is not always clear who was doing what and how much independence a particular woman actually had. Still, at least for the period between her marriages, it would seem as though the woman ran the business.[20] In 1771 there was at least one other woman, the widow Borup, and in 1801 there were four other women, all widows, who paid taxes on their printing businesses. In addition, four women, all widows, were listed as paying taxes as bookbinders. All of these women (except for Elisabeth Christine Berling) paid either one-quarter or one-half portion in taxes, the title difference seemingly irrelevant to their tax liability. But Berling spanned both periods and paid three portions, probably on her brewing rather than her publishing business. Because the Berling publishing business still exists, most information is available on her, but because her family was so famous, she should not be taken as representative. It is evident that the Berling and Godiche women were running their own businesses. Even T. Vogel-Jørgensen grudgingly concedes that Elisabeth Berling was "competent" and that she ran the firm with "understanding, judgment, daring, and authority."[21]

When Elisabeth Christine died in 1801, her sons had the property on Pilestræde assessed, prior to probate. There is a six-page description of the property, which stretched through from Pilestræde to Gammel Mønt, was four stories, and had at least three kitchens, plus the brewery. It was valued at 29,000 *rigsdaler*. When the property was bought in 1764, it had been valued at 11,500 *rigsdaler*.[22] That it more than doubled in value during this period is obviously due partly to the "good times" of the late eighteenth century, but certainly also attests to the maintenance of the property. It was not allowed to deteriorate, and, for this, its owners, including Elisabeth Christine, deserve credit.

Marie Martine Bonfils—brewer

The number of master guild brewers may have been capped at a hundred and included only men, but between 1740 and 1830, at least sixty-six women had some sort of official contact with government authorities as brewers. About two-thirds of these women were widows who carried on their husbands' businesses. (There is no information about the marital status of the remaining third.) Elisabeth Christine Berling may have been one of the most successful of these women, but she was far from unique. At least twenty female brewers paid self-employment taxes in 1771 and 1801, most often two portions, not a small amount, attesting to the perceived earning capability of this profession.

One of these women was Marie Martine Bonfils. When her husband Philibert died in 1773, Marie was allowed to continue his brewing business at the property on Springgade (now Pilestræde). Marie Martine was forty-two; she had seven children still at home. Her oldest child, Henrich, aged twenty-two, had already left home and established himself as a wine merchant. He agreed to allow his mother the continued use of his father's property, including the brewing license.[23] Maybe he should not have done so, because Henrich went bankrupt in 1784. (Of course, maybe

Fig. 4.4. Page from minutes of the *Bryggerikommission.* August 28, 1798. The eleventh and twelfth lines of text speak of "Mad. Bonfils and her son wine merchant Joseph Bonfils." Danish National Archives, Copenhagen.

if he had controlled the entire estate, he would have lost that as well.) At the time, he was doing business with his mother, but was not in business with her. He had been storing wine at her house, and she was onsite when the bankruptcy assessors came to check on Henrich's property. When he died, thirteen years later (1797), his estate was worth only 100 *rigsdaler.* It included nine pipes, worth a total of 9 *rigsdaler,* and a civilian militia uniform with hat, worth 8 *rigsdaler,* but no wine. He was survived by his wife, Petronelle, and two young daughters; his younger brother, Joseph, was named as the girls' guardian. What eventually happened to Petronelle is unknown, but she did not take over the wine business. Joseph did.[24]

Marie Martine's brewery, however, continued to flourish. For some reason, the property was finally probated in 1788, fifteen years after Philibert's death. At the time, it was valued at 19,875 *rigsdaler.* According to law, the widow (Marie Martine) received half of the estate's value, 9,937.50 *rigsdaler*, and the remaining half was split among seven of her eight children. (Henrich was not included in this because he had been paid off earlier, in a futile attempt to prevent his bankruptcy.) According to law, each son received twice as much as each daughter.[25] Joseph, the next oldest son (age twenty-four in 1788), had married Catarine Ratz, whose widowed mother, Sidse Olsdatter, owned and ran an inn in Frederiksberg, just outside the Copenhagen city walls. (Catarine's father, Georg Ratz, had also had a catering business.) Joseph continued his father's profession as a wine merchant but apparently was also in business with his mother's brewery. At any rate, a Brewery Commission investigation of August 28, 1795, refers to "Mad. Bonfils and her son, wine merchant Joseph Bonfils," which would imply that they were somehow working together but gives Marie pride of place with the first listing.[26]

Brewers and wine merchants were two separate occupations; brewers paid considerably more in self-employment taxes than did wine merchants. The Bonfils seniors, Philibert and then Marie Martine, paid three portions in self-employment tax from 1763 to 1778; from 1795 to 1801, Marie Martine paid only two portions. Of course, during this later period, after Philibert's death, the business had been split. Still, Marie Martine paid considerably more on her brewery than the one-half portion Joseph was charged as a wine merchant in 1801.[27]

In 1788, the brewery building on Springgade was valued at 12,000 *rigsdaler*, and in 1830 it was sold for 19,500 *rigsdaler*. Marie Martine died in 1804, and Joseph died even earlier, in 1801. Neither of the two Bonfils listed in the 1830 city directory lived at the Springgade address when the building was sold, so it is not known what happened to the rest of Joseph's siblings. In any case, Marie Martine ran a successful brewery for thirty years after her husband's death.

The Bonfils story seems to be one of an expansion of business interests through different avenues involving alcohol. The mother had a brewery; the sons were wine merchants. Their in-laws (the Ratz family) ran an inn and had connections with the Bonfils' business. At least two of Joseph's sons (he and Catarine had nine children) also spent time with their maternal grandmother at her inn. This represents a different form of "family economy." Although the family worked together, the separate households maintained independent businesses. This, I would suggest, reflects the general western pattern of independent nuclear families.

An interesting footnote to this story is that the Bonfils, at least the Bonfils seniors, were Catholic. Marie Martine left money to the Catholic Church in her will. Yet, despite the official Lutheranism of the country, there was no hindrance to the Bonfils' ability to conduct business. Non-Lutherans (Catholics, Jews, and other Protestants) were tolerated as long as they maintained accessible records and paid taxes.

Johanne Wadum Black Erichsen—merchant

The "palmy days" of the late eighteenth century were completely dependent on overseas trade. Historian Jens Vibæk concludes that "overseas trade was the main pillar in the economic structure of the 18th century. ... It was wholesale trade and shipping which brought us our wealth."[28] Wholesale trade and shipping were closely intertwined. Part of what defined a "wholesaler" or "merchant" (*grosserer*) was that one owned a ship or a share in a ship. When the Merchants Association (*Grosserer-Societetet* or GS) was founded in 1742, it included only "registered wholesalers." To be registered, one had to have "citizenship" (*borgerskab*) as a wholesaler *and* had to own at least some share in a ship. In 1790, when GS formalized its structure and hired an executive director, there were sixty-eight registered wholesalers in the city of Copenhagen, of whom thirty-nine signed GS' reorganization plan. By 1800, the numbers had grown to eighty wholesalers, forty-nine of whom were now members of GS.[29] There is a membership list from 1772 in GS' minute book. Of the forty-eight members, three were women, all widows—Widow Cicilia Jørgensen & Company, Franz Hinr. Kreutzfeld's Widow, and J.P. Schellenbeck's Widow. Although these names never showed up again and none of these women signed any of the documents, including meeting minutes, they were listed along with the men, with no visual distinctions.[30]

In 1771, three women paid taxes as wholesalers—Catarina Gustmeyer (or Gustmejer) (of whom more later), Cicilia Jørgensen, and Mrs. Severine Kreusfelt (or Kreutzfeld). All three were widows whose husbands had been members of GS. Thirty years later, in 1801, tax records listed eighty-nine people paying taxes as wholesalers, including two women—Charlotte Sophie Falck, a forty-three-year-old widow who was in business with her son and paid two portions in tax, and Margretha Elisabeth Perch, the forty-six-year-old widow of Jens Perch. Jens Perch, a tea merchant whose firm still exists, was an active member of GS; his widow continued the firm. This list does not include the firm of C.S. Black's Widow & Co., which paid taxes in 1801 as a landlord owning three warehouses on Christianshavn but was definitely in the wholesale business as well. The Widow Black (Johanne Wadum) was no longer alive in 1801; she had died the previous year, but the firm was continued by her second husband (Erich Erichsen) in her first husband's name.

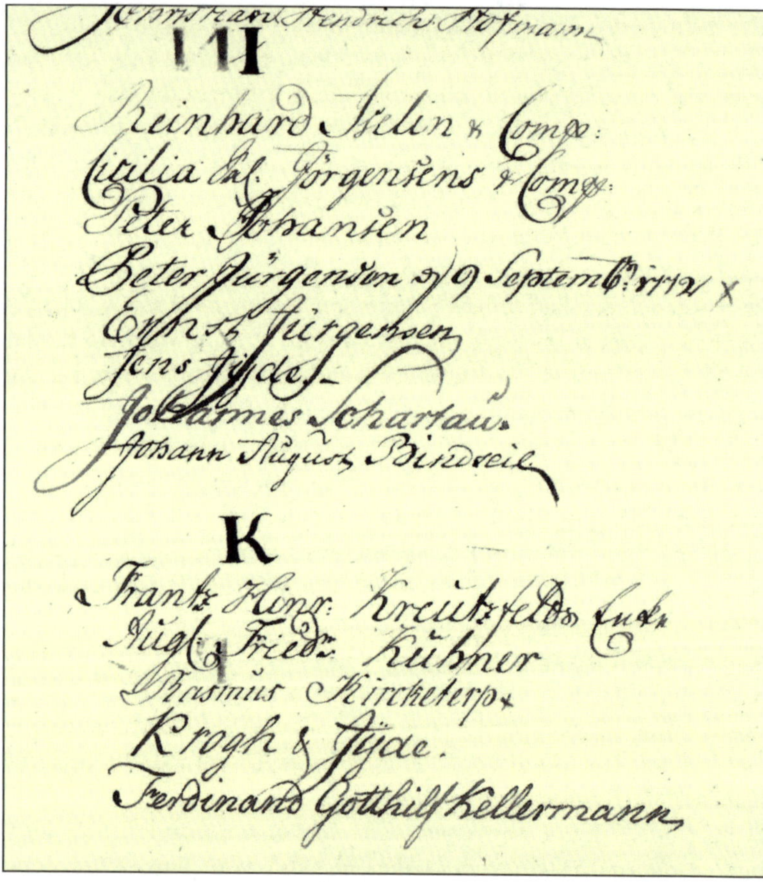

Christian Hendrich Hofmann

I

Reinhard Iselin & Comp:
Cicilia Sal: Jørgensens & Comp:
Peter Johansen
Peter Jürgensen d. 9 Septemb: 1772 x
Erich Jürgensen
Jens Tyde
Johannes Schartau
Johann August Bindseil

K

Frantz Hinr: Kreutzfelds Enke
Aug: Fried: Kühner
Rasmus Kirketerp
Krogh & Tyde.
Ferdinand Gotthilf Kellermann

Fig. 4.5. Page from *Grosserer-Societetets Forhandlingprotokol*, listing Cicilia Sal. Jørgensens & Comp (second name under "I") and Frantz Hinr. Kreutzfelds Enke (first name under "K"), 1772. The Danish Business Archives, Århus.

Although no one (male or female) was listed as paying taxes specifically as a ship owner, perhaps because they were all assumed to be wholesalers (*grosserere*), there were 191 "skippers" (*skipper*), all men, and 116 captains, including six women. It is not apparent to what degree these people may also have owned the ships, although they almost certainly had control over cargoes. There were also fifteen "agents," including one woman (what kind of agent is not specified).[31]

The firm C.S. Black's Widow & Co. ran several advertisements in *Adresseavisen* at the end of the eighteenth century. *Adresseavisen* was a Copenhagen newspaper that came out several times a week and carried an eclectic mix of official and theater notices, ship traffic, and advertisements for just about everything. People were both looking for and offering jobs, looking for and offering places to stay—both single rooms and apartments—offering all kinds of things to rent and sell, from bed linens and masquerade costumes (also for children) to cargo space. Most ads do not give names but just list addresses.[32] The advertisements of C.S. Black's Widow & Co. were fairly unusual in that respect, since they did give a company name. The company advertised overseas goods for sale. On January 9, 1801, for instance, cotton goods were offered for sale from the ship *Marianne,* as well as space on ships sailing both to and from the Danish West Indies.[33]

It is also apparent through the advertisements that the Erichsens maintained family connections with West Indian planters. In 1790, C.S. Black's Widow and Company advertised in both *Berlingske Tidende* and *Adresseavisen,* looking for anyone having business with or owed money by Lucas Benners, Jr., a planter who had died on St. Croix.[34] Benners' son, Isaac (now living in Copenhagen), had married into Erich Erichsen's sister-in-law's family. This shows the close intermingling of families within the same social circles, connections that could span the Atlantic Ocean. The Widow Black's firm owned ships engaged in transport to and from the West Indies, probably including slaves as well as sugar.[35] And at some point, Erich Erichsen obtained ownership of a sugar planation on St. Croix, named *Whim.*

The Widow C.S. Black was also listed in the 1801 tax records as owning three warehouses on Christianshavn and paying three and one half portions in self-employment tax, a very considerable amount. She was not listed as living on Christianshavn. In fact, the 1801 census has no record of any Black (or Blach).

However, Christen Schaarup Blach (or Black) was well-known in GS. His father, Oluf Blach, was one of its founders in 1742. The son, Christen Schaarup (C.S.), was a member of GS's three-man executive body from 1776 until his death in 1781. He was also a director in *Asiatisk Compagni* and a member of the board of The Royal Islandic-Finnmark Trade Association. In 1768, the thirty-three-year-old C.S. married twenty-one-year-old Johanne Wadum, who, when C.S. died in 1781, then became "C.S. Black's widow," retaining control of her husband's property until she remarried.

Eighteen months after C.S.'s death, Erich Erichsen, an employee in C.S.' firm, married the boss's widow, Johanne, and took over the house and the firm—an import-export merchant shipping company, now continued under the name of C.S. Black's Widow & Co. At this point, the property was probated; Johanne received half, about 20,000 *rigsdaler* and her two children with C.S. received the other half, split so that her son received twice as much as his sister, as was common.[36]

C.S. Black's Widow & Co. was a highly successful firm. After the 1795 fire devastated much of Copenhagen and the original Black house, Erichsen replaced it with a huge mansion on Kongens Nytorv. The new house was easily one of the grandest in the city; it still exists today and serves as the headquarters of Denmark's largest bank, *Den danske Bank*. It is three stories high, with a cellar under the entire building and a copper roof. The façade facing Kongens Nytorv has six Ionic columns topped with plaster figures, which are still there. The interior was decorated with stucco ceilings, painted leather paneling on the walls, gilded bas-reliefs, mirrors, mahogany trim, Grecian columns, built-in closets, and oil paintings. In 1804, the property was valued at 28,500 *risgdaler*.[37]

By 1797, C.S. Black's Widow & Co. owned the third-largest private shipping company in Denmark, with thirteen ships and a total carrying capacity of 1,422 *kommercelæster*. Although the shipping business ran into hard times during the Napoleonic Wars, Erichsen was able to transfer his primary business into money lending, where he was, again, highly successful, the Danish state being one of his main clients. Meanwhile, Johanne had died in 1800, but Erichsen continued to run the firm under his dead wife's name.[38]

It is admittedly hard to sort this one out. An earlier historian, Albert Fabritius, is convinced that, of course, Johanne Wadum Black Erichsen had nothing to do with running the company; it was all handled by Erichsen,

Fig. 4.6. Erichsen's Mansion, Kongens Nytorv, Copenhagen. Copenhagen City Museum.

but his only evidence is implicit and circumstantial. Because Erichsen had such a flourishing company after the death of his wife, Fabritius seems to assume that Erichsen must have run the company before Johanne died as well.[39] But why continue with *her* name? Continuing the firm under the name of "Black and Company" would make sense. The Blacks were well-known in wholesale and shipping circles, and one would want to continue with the good will of the earlier company. But why change the name to "C.S. Black's Widow" unless, at some point between the death of her first husband and her remarriage, Johanne was actually managing the company herself?[40] If this were the case, why automatically assume that she relinquished all control when she remarried? Maybe there was a partnership between the spouses.[41]

The following evidence is equally circumstantial but is offered as a different *possibility*. Johanne Wadum was born in Ålborg; her father was a retail grocer (*købmand*). It is not known if the family moved to

Copenhagen together or if Johanne moved on her own. There were two other Wadums listed in the 1787 census in Copenhagen—Owe, age thirty-nine, grocer, and Christen Hee, age fifty-one, a secretary and headmaster for the Royal Orphanage. But there were also still two Wadums in Ålborg that same year—Peder, age forty-two, who was a clergyman, and Claus, age thirty-six, who ran a school. If these families were all somehow related, then there is no doubt that Johanne came from a middle-class background. Middle-class girls often received an education commensurate with that of their brothers, as fathers expected them to be helpmeets for their future husbands.[42] This would lead to an assumption that Johanne was *capable* of carrying on the family business, although that does not necessarily prove that she did so. Marrying into the Black family would have meant a considerable step up socially.

It is clear that when C.S. Black died in 1781, *someone*, presumably Johanne, changed the company name to "C.S. Black's Widow & Co." It is also possible that Erichsen, in an early example of product branding, decided to continue the firm with the well-known name of "Black," although that still does not explain why the term "Widow" continued to be used—*after* their marriage in 1784 and even after her death in 1800. This choice reverses the more common pattern of a widow disappearing into the name of her second husband or her son. For example, Mrs. Kreutzfeld disappeared as Franz Hinrich Kreutzfeld's widow when she married Marius Gotthard Holm, also a member of GS.[43] Similarly, when her husband Laurentius Nicolas Cramer died in 1796, the Widow Cramer announced to her associates that the firm would continue in her sons' names, as "Cramer and Sons." She signed the document "H.M. sal. [widow] Cramer."[44] It would, of course, be equally interesting to know to what degree these women had been or continued to be involved in their husbands' businesses, but we know even less about them than about the Wadum-Black-Erichsen connection.

One final point is that in 1784, which was after Wadum and Erichsen had married, the signatures of both appear in GS' minute book, as "C.S. Blacks Enke" and "E. Erichsen" (see figure below). This is the only time that both names appear. After this, "C.S. Black's Widow & Co." was signed if it was on behalf of the company, but "E. Erichsen" when he signed as chair or member of the board. (Both formulations would seem to be in Erichsen's hand.) But at one point, when they were newly married, both names appear. Perhaps this indicated a partnership?[45]

Fig. 4.7. Erich Erichsen,
painted by Stein von Groeger, 1821.
Den Danske Bank, Copenhagen.

Further obfuscating the issue is the fact that the 1787 census, which has no listing for either Black or Blach, listed Johanne with her maiden name, Wadum, as living with her husband, Erich Erichsen, who was, of course, listed as head of household. The name Wadum would have been

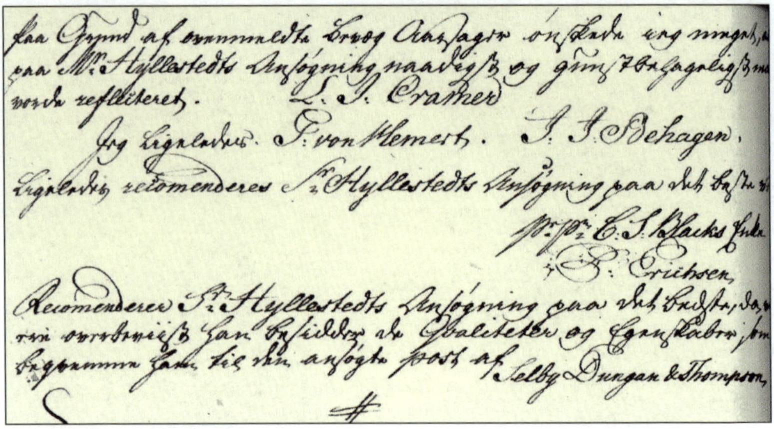

Fig. 4.8. Signatures of "C.S. Black's Widow" and "E. Erichsen," Grosserer-Societetet, *Forhandlingsprotokol, 1774–1790*, p. 166, 1784. The Danish Business Archives, Århus.

given by one of the spouses. One can certainly understand a woman reverting to her father's name in her second marriage (or indeed, never changing her name, which was common at the time), but why carry on the business as her first husband's widow? One would need to find the original company papers to sort this out. Meanwhile, there remains the intriguing possibility that this is an example of a widow who successfully ran her dead husband's business.

Johanne died suddenly in 1800, at the age of fifty-one. The death record lists the cause of death as "apoplexy," which could mean a stroke or simply that the death happened suddenly and was not the result of a long illness.[46] She was buried in Assistens Cemetery, probably in what is now referred to as the "historic" section. Erich lived to be eighty-five and never remarried. (See Appendix 4.2 for more on Erich's story.)

Catarina Gustmeyer—ship owner and timber merchant

Madame Catarina Gustmeyer (or Gustmejer), née Sprich (1710–1773), was a merchant and ship owner who specialized in supplying the Danish navy with timber. For several years, her firm held a monopoly on timber deliveries. This would have been of major importance, considering the size of the Danish navy. Her monopoly was successfully challenged in 1762 by Andreas Bodenhoff, who simply offered a lower price.[47] Nonetheless, in 1771, her firm was still highly successful, and Madame Gustmeyer paid three portions in self-employment tax as a wholesaler and timber merchant. The company, Gustmeyer and Bargum (Catarina's son-in-law), also owned a warehouse on Christianshavn but paid no taxes on it, although in 1776, the building was assessed at 1,300 *rigsdaler.* and said "to be in good condition."[48] In 1772, she sent a ship to the Virgin Islands with provisions to help the islands, which had been devastated by a hurricane. The implication was that this was a donation, although there is no proof of that.[49]

With her son-in-law, Bargum, Gustmeyer was also one of the founders of the Danish Guinea Company, a classic triangle trade operation. Ships were supposed to sail from Denmark to the coast of Guinea, in Africa, buy gold, ivory, and slaves, which would then be transported across the Atlantic to the Danish West Indies, where they would be exchanged for raw sugar to carry back to Denmark. The firm invested in a sugar refinery in Copenhagen as well as in three ships. For whatever reason, Catarina pulled out of the Danish Guinea Company shortly after it started, although Bargum continued, albeit not very successfully. In 1775, he was forced to flee the country to avoid his creditors and died around 1800, perhaps in France.[50]

The Gustmeyers lived in the luxurious style common for wealthy Copenhageners of the time. They bought a building on Ved Stranden, a street in downtown Copenhagen across from the royal palace. The building stretched through to the street behind. It was a two-story building with a balcony with a wrought iron fence. Inside, the rooms had tiled floors, stucco ceilings, and leather-paneled walls. In 1771, it was valued at 15,000 *rigsdaler.*[51]

Catarina's husband, Carl Hieronimus, had also been a merchant who had immigrated from Straslund; he was involved in currency exchange and timber. After he died in 1756, his widow, Catarina, inherited his business and continued to run it for the next fifteen years. It is likely that she also expanded it; at any rate, there is evidence that she decided both to go into business with her son-in-law and then to leave that business when she apparently began to mistrust him. After her death in 1773, the business was continued as Madame Gustmeyer and Son (this was Friderich, her son, not her dubious son-in-law). The various firms with which the Gustmeyers were involved provide good examples of the diversity of endeavors that could hide under the title of "merchant" or "ship owner." As ships plied the oceans, they transported a variety of goods, depending on what was available and seemed profitable at the time. This story also provides evidence of the possibilities and success available for women in this business.

Frederica Louise Ernst—factory owner and West Indian agent

All the women discussed so far were widows who took over and continued their husbands' businesses. Frederica Louise Ernst, on the other hand, was never married and remained single her entire life. Her father was an architect and contractor, active in city politics, so while she might have inherited money from him, she did not take over his business. By the time she was forty-four, Frederica had received permission to control her own funds. At that time, she owned part interest in a warehouse, ships, and a sugar plantation on St. Croix. She was probably also involved in the slave trade.[52]

In 1765, now fifty-one years old, Frederica applied to the royal Commerce Department for permission to start a factory to clean flax and extract linseed oil from the seeds. The department's response was that, since she had already received permission to control her own funds (been emancipated), she did not need the Commerce Department's permission. She was, according to the Commerce Department, "an intelligent and industrious woman." Ernst's factory had thirty-seven cleaning machines, hand-operated by nine cleaners, one sorter, and one "master."[53]

Unfortunately, Ernst's "industriousness" did not have a happy ending. In 1772, she tried, apparently unsuccessfully, to call in her loans. Six years later, while again trying to recoup her loans, she complained that her "money has remained fruitlessly in the West Indies for the past 17 years." When she died in 1781, she apparently had little left.[54] Nonetheless, Frederica Louise Ernst lived to be sixty-seven years old, all the while supporting herself on the proceeds from a flax factory and the West Indian trade. Although she may have had cash flow problems towards the end of her life, one does not get the impression that she was starving. She was another successful woman business manager.

Else Fenger—factory owner

There is a story, told through the generations in Else Fenger's family, that when her husband died in 1774, she approached her very wealthy merchant brother, Niels Brock, for a loan to keep her husband's soap factory going. Brock responded that he would advance her the money if she would end her sons' studies and engage them in "honest work" instead. Her response, according to family legend, was a forceful negative. "No, as sure as my name is Else, in no way will I do that. If it should cost me my last [silver] sweater button, they will remain at their studies." The story continues that Else approached another wealthy merchant, Christensen, for the loan. When he asked about collateral, she responded that "the only collateral I have is my honest face." Christensen then responded that he would lend her money, "on the basis of your honest face."[55] He did, and Else continued the soap factory quite successfully for the next thirty-seven years. Else's seven surviving sons all continued their studies, becoming a clergyman, an accountant, two landowners, a regimental surgeon, a professor of surgery—and Johannes, who continued the soap factory. The story says nothing about her two daughters, who both eventually married the same man—successively—Mouritz With, a captain in the merchant marine.[56]

There are, of course, a few "issues" with this delightful story. Why did Else need the money in the first place? Were there problems with the soap factory? Or with some of her husband Peter's other investments? He had also been a wholesaler in flax, coal, and wine, engaged in shipping and exchange. Did Brock know something about his brother-in-law's investments that his widow did not? How did Christensen fit into all of this? Were there issues between him and Brock? Intrigues, intrigues! Else's answer to Christensen about a lack of collateral is also disingenuous—unless they all knew that Peter had actually run the property into the ground. After all, there was the soap factory itself and the house on Christianshavn.

Whatever the reality of the relationships and Peter Fenger's finances, in 1778, four years after his death, his property was auctioned off. Else was able to hold on to the house and the soap factory, at Strandgade 55, on Christianshavn. Three years later, in 1781, Peter Borre left the firm he had started with Peter Fenger, which ended the firm of Borre & Fenger. Yet Else persevered, and the soap factory continued to support her and her family.

Nicolai Meinert (1791–1877), two of whose sisters married two of Else's sons (Rasmus and Johannes), wrote of her in his memoirs:

> Else Fenger did not sell the property, neither did she get rid of any of the things that her husband had left her. She remained in the house alone, as before, with horses and carriages, a driver, and

Fig. 4.9. Else Fenger, painted by Ulrich Ferdinandt Beenfeldt, 1780. The Danish Royal Library, Copenhagen.

> servant. She kept living in a splendid manner, yet she understood how to arrange things so that she could educate all her children, and when she died, she was moderately wealthy.[57]

Meinert attributed Else's success to "the times," but did admit that she understood how to make use of the good times. "She carried on her own

Fig. 4.10. The Fenger Family, painted by Ulrich Ferdinandt Beenfeldt, 1769. The Danish National Museum, Copenhagen.

correspondence and had insight into the accounts. No one can deny that she was vigilant, active, and careful in her own interests."[58]

Else's granddaughter, Molly, remembered her grandmother as "very hospitable; she ran a comfortable house, where everyone was welcome," although she also recalled that Else's sons "sometimes felt oppressed by her decisiveness."[59] It is rare that we have personal memories like these from two hundred years ago. They certainly support the idea of a strong woman who took active charge of her own life. Did she, perhaps, also run her children's lives? In any case, Else ran the business she inherited from her husband very successfully, enabling her to support and educate her children in a manner she chose.

Anette Lucie Benedicte Linde—schoolkeeper

At the turn of the eighteenth to the nineteenth century in Copenhagen, there were well over two hundred private schools for girls. These ran the gamut from small daycare centers and homes catering to very young children under the age of eight, to large ladies academies that paralleled the new *realskoler* (high schools) for boys, teaching academic subjects in what we today would consider college preparatory courses. We know this from two major sources: applications for permission to establish and run private, proprietary schools, and reports on schools that were already open. In 1814 the Danish government introduced compulsory education for all children—girls as well as boys—from age seven until they were confirmed, usually around age fourteen. The city of Copenhagen responded by surveying those schools that already existed and using them as a basis for the city's school system.[60]

One of the largest academies was owned and run by Anette Linde, who opened a private, proprietary school for girls in 1787, when she was twenty-four years old and probably newly married.[61] The school catered to girls aged seven to seventeen, to whom it taught writing, arithmetic, history, geography, French, German, English, religion (Lutheranism), and handwork. Reading is absent from this list because it was assumed that the girls already knew how to read before they started at this school. The school was divided into five classes, and the school day ran from nine in the morning until two in the afternoon. Anette Linde was married to Georg Christopher Lorentz Linde, a master goldsmith and also a member of the city's 32 Men, the Copenhagen City Council. The couple had at least two daughters, Vilhelmine Charlotte and Christine Laurentze, who inherited and continued the school after their mother died in 1815. Two years later, when visited by Professor Brorson for the Copenhagen Board of Education, the school had one hundred students, which made it one of the largest private schools in the city. In 1830, the school still had ninety students, sixteen of whom were paid for by the royal family.[62]

These private girls schools have had a bad reputation in Danish school history, partly because Johan Ludvig Heiberg, a renowned Danish playwright, and his wife Johanne Luise, both made fun of the schools. Johan Ludvig wrote a play called *The April Fools* (*Aprilsnarrene*) in 1828, ridiculing girls schools; his wife later wrote a scathing attack on their uselessness. Nevertheless, roughly 250 private, tuition-charging schools for girls operated in the city of Copenhagen. It is hardly likely that parents would have continued to send their daughters to and pay for such schools if they were completely useless. Natalie Zahle (1827–1913), a well-known pioneer of higher education for girls, remembered her parents choosing between the Copenhagen Daughters School of 1791 (*Døttreskolen af 1791*) and Madame Linde's "fancier, very French school" for her to attend. They eventually chose the former.[63]

One girl whose parents did decide to send her to Madame Linde's school was Catharina Magdalena Frohbøese (her married name); she attended from 1806 to 1808, when she was fourteen to sixteen years old. The training she received there enabled her to work as a governess until she got married to a captain in 1814, when she was twenty-two. The next year she opened up her own private girls school when she received permission from the Copenhagen Board of Education (*Direktionen for Almue- og Borgerskolevæsenet*) to teach writing, arithmetic, and religion to girls up to age fourteen. In 1821, she had twenty-one girls enrolled in her school, and the curriculum had broadened to include German, French, history, geography, and drawing.[64]

It is hard to know exactly how many girls went to these schools, but I estimate that at least half the school-age population had some formal schooling outside the home. For girls, that meant mostly private for-tuition schools run by independent schoolkeepers who owned their own schools. Few schools were as large as Madame Linde's and her daughters' school, but all these women ran their own schools as their own businesses. Since we know that Madame Linde's school existed from its inception in 1787 at least until 1830, a period of forty-three years, it should be considered a success and its founder and her daughters to be successful business managers.

Madame Linde is also a prime example of the need to change the standard narrative of women's involvement in a family economy. Anette and her husband Georg Linde both lived and worked at the same address—Raadhusstræde number 8. Georg was a master goldsmith, the chair of the goldsmith's guild, and a member of the Copenhagen City Council. His wife ran her own business separately from Georg's. Managing a day and boarding school for about a hundred girls, it is hard to imagine that Anette had any time left over to help in her husband's shop. The traditional women's history narrative would see Anette and her daughters helping the male head of household in his goldsmith business. Instead, the three women in the family worked in a separate business of schoolteaching and -keeping. The daughters eventually inherited their mother's business, not their father's.

The women whose stories have been chronicled in this chapter were all successful in running their own businesses. These businesses were relatively large and contributed to the thriving economy in late eighteenth-century Copenhagen. With only two exceptions (Ernst and Linde), these women were all widows continuing their husbands' firms; they were capable and successful in these endeavors. They represent the possible. It was possible for a woman to maintain her own businesses; she did not need "cover" from a husband, a father, or sons. In some cases, she might even do better on her own, without male help or other male involvement (cf. Marie Martine Bonfils and possibly Else Fenger). Indeed, sons often had to wait for their mothers to die before they could inherit the family business. In some cases, it would appear that sons chose not to wait but rather to set up separate businesses on their own, sometimes working with mothers, at other times in completely different fields. Else Fenger, of course, insisted on this for six of her seven surviving sons. In some cases, women inherited from mothers, as did Elisabeth Christine Berling from her mother, Anna Magdalena Godiche, or the Linde daughters from their mother.

These women all demonstrate the possibility of a different life trajectory. Women could work with husbands, fathers, or sons in a family economy. *Or* they could work on their own, separate from male relatives, but sharing living space and probably also economic resources. This mirrors a pattern with which we are familiar today—the two-income family.

Chapter Five

Married Women–and their Husbands

> What happiness for a man, who could not claim to live without working, to have such an admirable girl, a worthy *helper* in life in the truest meaning of the word. Since with her beneficial and honorable work she will also be able to earn her part of the common household livelihood, her care and domesticity will do very well.[1]

When M. Sibbern wrote this, he represented a shift that was taking place in women's perceived economic role towards more domesticity. This quote comes from an 1806 article on "Girls Schools," in which Sibbern attacked the growing trend of educating girls. "They must learn to think, people say! Well enough, but they must especially learn to think about what will be their future call and duty as housewives and their husbands' helpers [feminine form] and truest friends [also feminine form] in everything that concerns his domestic welfare."[2] In other words, girls were to be trained to act as their husbands' helpmates. Men needed wives who could contribute to the family's work, but the wives needed no more education than their ability, "as housewives," to run a good household.

The new ladies academies in Copenhagen and on Christianshavn were emphasizing the "scientific" subjects of history, natural science, mathematics, and geography—subjects Sibbern and others considered superfluous.[3] Women, these writers believed, worked with husbands in what has come to be known as a "family economy," in which the husband made the shoes, for example, and his wife sold them. She probably kept the records and managed the house as well. The family, or household, presented an integrated urban economic unit in which both husband and wife were necessary but played very separate and distinct roles, in a pattern that has come to be called "separate spheres."

When rhetoric on a topic begins to heat up, this usually indicates that a change is taking place. After all, there is no need for passionate discussions on topics on which all agree. Social and economic changes in the mid- to late eighteenth century gave rise to demands for more education, for girls as well as for boys. The question as regarded girls, however, was just how much and what sort of education would be most advantageous. The subjects taught in the new girls academies, often established by parents, paralleled those taught to their brothers in the new *real* schools, or *gymnasia*. Writers such as Sibbern, however, thought this a waste of time. Women had no use for such information, these authors believed, since all they would do would be to help their husbands in a domestic economy. This reflected a change from an earlier reality in which women had worked co-equally with men, although not necessarily alongside them.

This research has shown that the early modern urban reality was much more complex than Sibbern assumed. Many married women worked on their own, in their own names, not as part of a family economy. Our perceptions have been skewed by looking back through a two-hundred-year period when prescriptions instructed women to remain in the house and be responsible for domestic reproduction. We have lost sight of both the reality that women have always worked throughout the economy and the fact that authors such as Sibbern reflected a prescription, a *desired* outcome, and not the reality.

Of the approximately three thousand women in my database, all of whose names I know, about 45 percent (ca. 1,350) were married and 20 percent were widows; the marital status of the remaining one-third is unknown. Refiguring the percentages only for those women whose marital status is known, then, 73 percent were married and 24 percent were widows. (The remaining 2 to 3 percent of women in both cases were mostly never married, with a small group who were separated from their husbands or divorced.) In either case, if about one-half of independent women working were married and working separately from their husbands, it is time to modify the narrative.

There are various ways to look at the married women who were working in the eighteenth and early nineteenth centuries. One can approach these women through the perspective of what they were actually doing. Although 80 percent were, not surprisingly, to be found in some area of the food industry, it is also clear that women could be found throughout the economy and were not excluded from any specific branches or occupations.

Another approach to this subject is from the perspective of husbands, both in terms of what husbands were or, in some cases, were not doing, but also an indication of families' socio-economic status. Women did tend to be ascribed male relatives' economic status. So, what were husbands doing? Were they engaged in the same or similar trades as their wives? Or did husbands do something completely different? This research has shown that only a handful of married women working on their own were in the same field as their husbands. Of these, there were, for example, one watchmaker family, a family brewing (and selling) beer, and one selling tobacco. There were also several school families (Engelsen and Tidemand, see chapter three). Several women who had market passes or permission to sell "domestic goods" (as opposed to foreign, overseas, or colonial goods) traveled with husbands or sold goods available in husbands' shops, as, for example, was the case with the Gianellis. Some women had permission to sell articles of clothing produced by themselves or by husbands who were tailors or dressmakers or who had small shops for the sale of linen or woolen goods. These couples were obviously in the same business, and each spouse's work complemented the other's. Some of these women traveled together with their husbands; some traveled alone. Rikke Furst had permission to travel "when her husband was absent," although the license, from 1826, said nothing about when or why he might be absent.[4]

But the overwhelming majority of married women with official government licenses were working in fields that had nothing to do with their husbands' jobs. In some cases, this was because of the nature of the work. Midwives were obviously in business for themselves, without regard to

Table 5.1

Married Women's Occupational Categories

Food and beverage production and distribution		1,071	80%
Military wives	640		
Street and market stalls	390		
Other	41		
Education		75	6%
Clothing production and distribution		55	4%
Other production and distribution		55	4%
Midwives		52	4%
Service, dancers, actors, etc.		36	3%
Other		3	>1%
Total		1,347	

NB: This list contains *only* those women whose marital status is known. The marital status of one-third of the women in my database is unknown, so the percentages may be somewhat skewed. Percentages are rounded up.

husbands' occupations. Husbands who were in the military or who were gone for long periods in the shipping industry, obviously could not include wives in a family economy. This still left a large number of women who were working at one job while their husband worked at another. Wives' earnings undoubtedly helped to support the family unit, as did husbands' earnings, but spouses were not necessarily working alongside each other in a family shop.

Looked at from the husbands' perspectives, most were in the military; it was their wives who automatically received permission to sell fruit on the streets. Of the remaining approximately two hundred husbands, there is no occupational information for sixty-three of them. About half of the husbands whose occupation is known were either master craftsmen or some other form of professional; only one-third were journeymen, workmen, or some other form of dependent employee. Gotleib Eichel, for instance, who was a wholesaler, had a wife, Frederikke, who received a royal privilege in 1820 to sew and sell women's clothing. Additionally, she was also given permission to teach women sewing.[5] Øllegaard Kroll's second husband, Karl Wilhelm Kroll, was a wigmaker. In 1801, Øllegaard received municipal permission to sell used clothes, copper, pewter, and other similar items.

What we see here, then, is a pattern of independent, middle-class men, men with "solid" jobs, whose wives were also working independently, outside of the husbands' businesses. Working wives were, of course, contributing to the total family income, but that does not negate the fact that wives were working on their own, not within a "family economy." This was not a group at the bottom of the social scale, either, but a group firmly in the middle. (See Appendix 5.1 for a list of job titles.)

Yet another way to look at these women is from the perspective of why they were working. Here we know much less. Insofar as they said anything in their applications, they always claimed to need work in order to support themselves and their families, often including several underage children. An obvious group of women who needed to work were those whose husbands were away from home, either in the military or in overseas trade. Copenhagen was, after all, both a military town and a large shipping port.

Johanne Svendsdatter Isaachson, a weaver, age forty-four, received permission from the city of Copenhagen, on May 2, 1803, to "weave all kinds of clothing." Her husband was a carpenter at Holmen, a naval base in town. The official letter commented that it was common to give such permission to military wives, who otherwise would have trouble supporting themselves.[6] Most of these women, as we have seen, received permission to peddle food on the city streets. Johanne, however, was given permission to weave and sell clothing. Marie Sophie Holm received a royal privilege in January 1820 to open a restaurant selling food and drink, "for persons not of the simple common class (*uden for den simple almuesklasse*)." Her husband, Ole Christian Holm, was a ship captain and presumably gone for long periods of time.[7]

In an unusual turnabout, Mette Katharine Farre, whose husband was just listed as "soldier," received a royal privilege in May 1816 to work as a pork butcher, as long as she paid taxes. The document also stated that, when her husband retired from the military, he would take over her license to carry on in the pork business.[8] Common to these permissions is an attempt to assure the economic maintenance of women who might otherwise have difficulty supporting themselves because their husbands were away.

Another group of married women who received official favor and municipal licenses were those whose husbands were "workers" (*arbejdsmænd*) or journeymen (*svende*). Here the assumption was that the husbands did not earn enough to support a wife and family. Sophie Amalia Høyer received a license from the city of Copenhagen in 1801 to sell fruit and white bread, because she "had no other way to support herself." Her husband, Christian Høyer, was listed as a workman, but there is no other information on him.[9] Beate Antinette Augusta Møller applied for permission to open a tea and coffee shop in 1821. Her husband, Christian Møller, was a journeyman bricklayer. She received permission from the city on April 6, 1821, as long as she paid taxes, allowed dancing only with prior police permission, and did not allow ongoing disorder![10]

The finding that most complicates the standard narrative is the large group of married women from professional or middle-class backgrounds who worked in fields wholly unconnected with those of their husbands. In 1822, Nicoline Cornelia Køpke received a royal privilege to bleach, sew, and embroider straw and silk hats and scarves, which she might then offer for sale, as long as she bought the necessary materials from officially sanctioned firms (in other words, guild-sanctioned and tax-paying firms) and paid self-employment tax on her earnings. Her husband, Peder Gødsen Køpke, was the head of an (educational?) institute.[11] Anne

Cathrine Neumann received a royal privilege in July 1815 to work as a ladies dressmaker (*modehandler*). Her husband, Trangott Neumann, was a master saddlemaker, whose work was profitable enough to enable him to pay one-quarter portion in self-employment tax in 1811, yet still his wife received permission to work.[12]

Marie Christine Drebolt, whose family was perhaps trying desperately not to slide down the economic scale, received two separate communal privileges—the first in 1825 to function as an innkeeper, and the second in 1829 to keep a small shop (*høker*). This second permit was returned to the city in 1835, when Marie Christine was sixty-seven. Meanwhile, her husband, Henrich Thomas Drebolt, a master house painter, also changed fields and became a customs official later in life.[13] The family would seem to have been doing quite well in 1801. According to the census that year, in addition to three children, Henrich had two painter apprentices; the family also kept a serving girl. What happened later is unknown. Similarly, Ane Marie Fensmark received permission in 1826 from the Copenhagen municipal government to sew women's clothes and then offer them for sale. Her husband, Simon Thomas Fensmark, was a free carpenter; he was trained as a turner and allowed to work as a master carpenter although he did not belong to a guild.[14]

Did these women work because the family needed the money? Did they work because they wanted some disposable income of their own? Or was working the acceptable thing to do? Everyone worked; why shouldn't they? Trying to sort this out is as difficult as it is to sort out why modern women work, so maybe this is the wrong question. If everyone works, maybe the question should be why some women did not work. It is past time to question the assumption that middle-class women retreated into the home and, by definition, did not work. It is obvious from this research that, for whatever reason or set of reasons, married women from all social groups in early modern Copenhagen were working, both within and outside the home, in a wide variety of occupations, both with and without their husbands.

Chapter Six

Concluding Thoughts

I was eating dinner in a restaurant recently, one of those places where the tables are so close together that you can hear everyone at the next table. I was discussing this book project with my restaurant companion. On my way out, the woman at the table next to mine stopped me and asked about my work. When I responded that I was working on a project concerning women in eighteenth-century Copenhagen who worked in their own names, not with husbands, fathers, or sons, her response was, "oh, how modern! They were early feminists." I smiled and walked out.

The important thing to note here is that women have *always* worked. The idea that women stayed at home, caring for the family while the husband was the sole breadwinner, is a construct whose fabrication can be dated to the nineteenth century. This belief was reinforced in the mid-twentieth century by the ideal of a stay-at-home mom with lots of children after the devastation of the Second World War. If such households had ever existed in reality, they were confined to a small group of successful, middle-class families. However, the *idea* was prevalent and continues to exist to this day—witness my neighbor at the restaurant.

Not only did women continue to work in the post-war economies, albeit often for less pay, but urban women had always worked. No one denies that rural women worked on farms, but city women have also worked as consistently as their country sisters. There is nothing new or unusual in this story, except that it has been hidden and we are only just beginning to uncover it.

When confronted with this fact, many people go on to assume that yes, of course, *widows* have worked; they would have carried on their husbands' businesses. And indeed, widows did make up a large percentage of urban working women, but working women were not exclusively widows. In eighteenth- and early nineteenth-century Copenhagen, only about one-quarter of legally working women were widows (see Chart 1.1), while almost three-quarters were married; a handful were single, either divorced or never married.

There was, however, a difference in the kinds of things widowed or married women were doing. Widows tended to be found in professional trades, such as printers, merchants, schoolkeepers, and in the building and metal trades. These women had obviously inherited jobs from deceased husbands. Married women were more often to be found in the food industry, an area more typically associated with women.

Chart 6.1

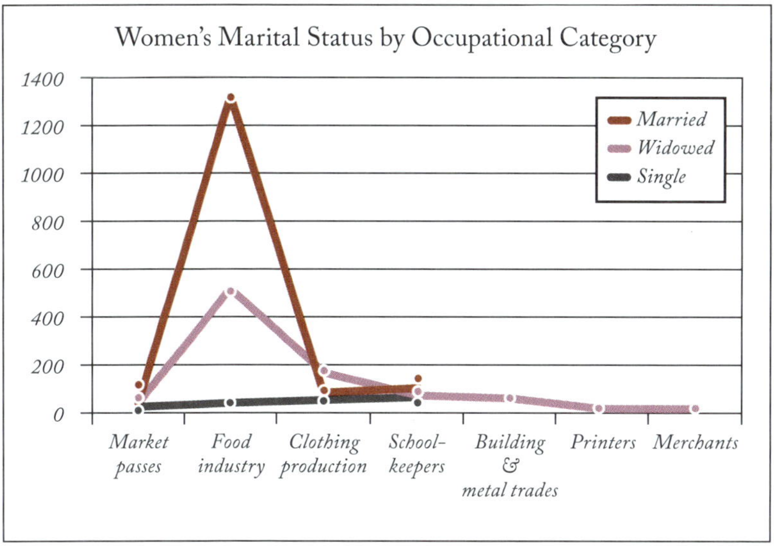

Moreover, this research illustrates that not only were married women working, but they were often working in occupations that were separate from and had nothing to do with their husbands. Obvious categories here are midwives and military wives. Because of the nature either of their own work (midwives) or of their husbands' (in the military), it is understandable that these spouses could not engage in so-called "family economies." The same would be true of women who were married to government employees (civil servants) or to men at sea, a large category in the Danish islands. Nevertheless, there was also a large number of women who could have worked with husbands but who did not. Perhaps the business was not large enough to engage the wife's services fully, or perhaps she was more familiar with another trade, or had started her own business prior to getting married. Although marriages tended to take place within similar professions since the families socialized with each other (as, for example, the Berling-Goddiche-Høpfner connection), this was not always the case. Anette Linde, discussed in Chapter Five, is a good example of a different pattern. Madame Linde owned and ran a boarding and a day school for girls, which she started the year she got married. Her husband was a master goldsmith, who owned the building where he and his wife and family lived, and which housed both their businesses. Georg Christopher Linde was a member of the Copenhagen City Council, so there is extant information about him, but this family was not unique. Wife and husband both ran professional businesses, situated in the same building, but otherwise separate and distinct from each other. It was a common pattern, one that has parallels in today's two-income families.

Women were to be found working throughout the economy. The only exclusions were in the military, government service, the clergy, and at sea. Women were everywhere else. It bears repeating that this pattern includes industries such as the building and metal trades and transportation where one does not ordinarily expect to find women. Neither laws nor regulations prohibited women from participating in any industry. Although guilds did not formally allow women as members, this did not, apparently, preclude women's activity within guild-controlled industries. Some industries may not have had many women, such as the shipping industry, where only three or four women owned shipping companies and six made either rope or sails, but that does not negate the fact that it

Table 6.1

Total Women Occupational Categories

Food and alcohol	1,881
Clothing	314
Production and distribution	175
Medicine/midwives	508
Education	245
Humanities	52
Landlords	15
Other services/titles	24
Building trades	45
Shipping	10
Misc/unknown	44
Total	3,313

was *possible* for women to work legally in that industry. This research has thus illuminated the legal possibilities that existed for women, even as women also engaged illegally, or unofficially, in several of these businesses as well. Customers or clients would not necessarily know the difference. The reality is that women were present and economically active.

So how is it that we find women throughout the economy, even in areas where we would not expect to find them? First, we need to remind ourselves that some of our expectations exist because we are looking through a filter that was not really there at the time—the domestic ideology of the nineteenth and twentieth centuries. Yet, even after moving the filter aside, it does seem to have been remarkably easy for women to participate in the late preindustrial economy in Denmark. There are some possible reasons for this.

First, the legal system smoothed the way for women. There was no effective coverture, so women were able to work legally throughout the economy. Additionally, and very importantly, the reality of *uskiftet bo* (unprobated estates) meant that women, and especially middle-class women, would grow up with the knowledge that they might inherit their husbands' businesses. It is quite clear that daughters in professional families learned the family trade and were expected to be able to continue the business if necessary. That many went into these businesses before they were widowed, while husbands were still alive, is also a reality. If a woman married within the same business, as did Karen Mariager, ropemaker, or Maria Catharina and Elisabeth Christine Godiche, printers, then the transition would have been simple and probably seamless. Although we do not know for sure, we can assume that these wives may well have helped their husbands with the business. This is, after all, the essence of the concept of the "family economy." Women who married into other fields, such as Johanne Wadum or Anette Linde, might have learned their husband's business (Wadum) or continued in a separate field (Linde), but in any case, they definitely had some education and probably already possessed basic knowledge about how to conduct a business.

Additionally, in hindsight we can see that this was a transitional economy, on the cusp of a change from a preindustrial, somewhat medieval, guild-dominated economy to a more modern, industrial, capitalist economy. Factories were already being established around Copenhagen, dependent on overseas colonial products such as sugar and cloth. Moreover, the royal government was making full use of opportunities to chip away at the constraining guild structures. It was thus possible for women to slip through and function within the interstices of these changes.

In understanding this process, we must also remember that these women were not working because they were early "feminists," as my restaurant neighbor supposed, but rather due to economic necessity. People worked to support themselves and their families. Women often said as much in their applications for business licenses and permits. They claimed the need to support underage children or incapacitated husbands, the need to keep the family going in the face of adversities such as "bad times" or spousal abandonment, or just the desire to stay clear of poor help. That women also enjoyed or found fulfillment in their work is a possibility that can not be denied. Neither Elisabeth Christine Berling, Else Fenger, nor Marie Martine Bonfils exhibited any interest in retiring, much to the possible chagrin of their sons. One can hope that they continued to receive something positive from their work, despite initially maintaining businesses because they and their families needed the financial resources.

Putting together this research has been somewhat like stitching a crazy quilt and trying to figure out how to fit the pieces together into a coherent whole. Since people at the time did not think women working was at all out of the ordinary, no one thought to collect information about their work in a systematic manner. It is thus up to the modern researcher to find the scattered bits and piece them together into an intelligible whole. Information about women working is available in any number of different places—applications for licenses, business licenses, tax records, municipal records, census records, city directories, bankruptcy and probate records, some guild records—and these sources all need to be checked and collated. Although it is rarely possible to describe the entire life trajectory of an individual woman, once pieced together, the snapshots of information can provide a representative picture.

It is time to revisit the traditional narrative of the "family economy." We can now all agree that women were working. This research has also shown that women worked outside the family structure as well as within it. Women in eighteenth- and early nineteenth-century Copenhagen were engaged in individual enterprises as they expanded their work to support themselves and their families into all branches of the economy. The Danish legal system of the time both allowed and encouraged these practices. Individual family units remained at the core of the economy, but they were units within which adult members contributed in a variety of ways, both as an integral part of a family business and as a contributing member of a family unit.

Appendices

Appendix 3.1: 1801 Self-Employment Tax Occupational Listings

Women

Occupation	Number
agent	1
auctioneer	3
baker	5
baker, of bread	2
baker, of cakes	1
baker, of tarts	1
banker	2
barber	3
billiard parlor keeper	1
blacksmith	1
boarding house host	4
book publisher	3
bookbinder	4
brewer	9
bricklayer	1
butcher	2
candlemaker	3
captain	6
cardmaker	1
carpenter	6
chair maker	1
clockmaker	1
clothing seller	2
confectioner	1
cooper	1
corduroy preparer	1
distiller	6
dyer	2
fish seller, of dried fish	1
flour seller	1
fruit seller	1
game seller	1
gardener	1
glazier	2
glitterer	1
goldsmith	1
greengrocer	2
grocer	2
hackney coachman	1
hardware storekeeper	3
ironmonger	1
jeweler	1
junk dealer	1
lace dealer	1
landlord	78
linen seller	2
locksmith	1
manufacturer	2
merchant	2
merchant/shopkeeper	3
miller	1
milliner	1
painter	1
pottery seller	3
publican	2
roofer	2
ropemaker	1
sailcloth dealer	4
sailmaker	1
sausage seller	1
shoemaker	9
shopkeeper, small	9

smith	2
soapmaker	2
starch dealer	1
starchmaker	1
stocking weaver	1
street paver	1
supercargo	1
surgeon	2
sutler	1
sword maker	2
tailor	4
tea handler	5
teashop owner	1
tobacco dealer	5
tobacco producer	1
tobacco roller	2
turner	1
wagonmaker	1
wheelwright	1
wine merchant	1

Men

accountant	1
acid producer, for soap	1
agent	4
anchor smith	3
apothecary	1
architect	3
armory, in charge of	1
artilleryman	1
assessor	5
assistant	1
auctioneer	10
auctioneer, owner	2
auditor	1
baker	61
baker, of bread	21
baker, of cakes	2
banker	3
barber, hair cutter	13
barber surgeon	11
bargeman	1
barometer maker	1
basket maker	3
beer tapster	504
bell founder	3
belt maker	2
billiard parlor keeper	19
blacksmith	13
bleacher	2
block maker	4
boarding house host	31
boatswain	1
book publisher	12
bookbinder	28
bookkeeper	2
bookseller	13
box maker	4
brewer	45
bricklayer	39
brickmaker	1
broker	21
brushmaker	4
builder	2
butcher	58
button maker	8
calico printer	9
calico seller	2
camphor producer	1
candlemaker	60

canvas producer	1
captain	79
carding brush maker	2
card maker	1
carpenter	169
carpet maker	1
cashier	2
caterer	8
cellist	1
chair maker	19
cheese seller	1
chemical production	1
chimneysweep	2
china repairer	2
chocolate maker	1
church official	1
clockmaker	43
clothing cutter	1
clothing maker	4
clothing seller	30
club host	5
coach builder	2
coast guard, member of	1
coffee dealer	4
coffee shop owner	6
collection agent	1
colonial goods seller	48
comb maker	5
confectioner	12
cooper	35
coppersmith	22
cork cutter	1
corset maker	2
courier	2
curate	3
dentist	1
designer	1
dispatcher	1
distiller	233
doctor	4
drummer	1
dyer	14
engineer	1
engraver	12
entrail seller	1
fabric maker	5
fire captain	1
firewood dealer	2
fishmonger	4
fish seller, of dried fish	13
flax beater	1
flax comber	1
flour dealer	15
footman	1
fringe maker	12
fruit seller	6
furniture dealer	2
furrier	9
garbage collector	3
gardener	11
gilder	4
glass cutter	2
glass dealer	9
glazier	21
glover	12
goldbeater	1
goldsmith	51
goldwire drawer	4
grain measurer	1
gravedigger	2
greengrocer	89
grocer	59
guild host	2
gunsmith	1
hackney coachman	13
hairdresser	3

hairdresser, ladies'	1
hardware storekeeper	16
hatter	13
horse dealer	1
innkeeper	217
inspector	2
instrument maker	8
ironmonger	5
jeweler	6
junk dealer	34
lace dealer	1
lacquer maker	1
landlord	323
lawyer	1
leather finisher	3
leather goods producer	2
lemon seller	1
linen seller	1
linen weaver	18
locksmith	39
lumber dealer	3
maltster	1
man of letters	1
managing clerk	6
manufacturer	20
meat dealer	7
mechanic	2
merchant	57
metalworker	1
miller	23
milliner	3
mirror maker	1
mirror seller	1
music printer	1
music seller	1
nailsmith	12
naval officer	4
needlemaker	8
nightsoil collector	2
office worker	1
optician	1
organ builder	3
organist	1
painter	42
parchment dealer	1
pattern maker	1
pen maker	1
perfume seller	1
pewterer	9
pigeon seller	1
pipemaker	1
plasterer	4
plumber	11
porcelain dealer	10
pork butcher	3
postman	1
pottery seller	29
professor	10
publican	4
purveyor	1
quartermaster	4
refiner	2
registrar	1
ribbon maker	2
roofer	3
ropemaker	12
saddle maker	23
sailcloth dealer	14
sail maker	6
sailor	1
sausage maker	1
sausage seller	1
schoolkeeper	3
schoolmaster	1
scrap dealer	4
scribe	1

sculptor	2	supercargo	1
sealmaker	5	surgeon	17
secretary	3	sutler	21
seller of toys, decorations	4	sword maker	3
sexton	2	tailor	224
shipbuilder	3	tailor, men's pants	2
shipyard foreman	1	tanner	26
shoemaker	287	tax collector	17
shopkeeper	172	tea dealer	54
shopkeeper, small	311	teashop owner	18
silk dealer	1	theater dancer	1
silk weaver	1	thread dealer	2
silverplater	1	threadmaker	1
skipper	189	ticket taker	1
smith	19	tobacco dealer	19
smoker	1	tobacco producer	9
soap dealer	1	tobacco roller	9
soap maker	2	translator	1
soldier	2	undertaker	4
sole maker	1	vinegar brewer	3
spice dealer	1	wagoner	39
spray maker	1	wagonmaker	2
spur maker	1	warehouse manager	1
stableman	8	watchman	1
starch dealer	1	water inspector	1
starch maker	4	weaver	4
steward	6	weigher	1
stocking maker	6	wheelwright	12
stocking weaver	4	wigmaker	40
stone mason	5	wine merchant	41
stove dealer	1	wood turner	27
sugar refiner	6	woodstove maker	2
sugar seller	1	worker	5

The total number listed here does not add up to the total of 6,207 records, because 340 names have no occupational listing and several people are listed only with noble or government titles.

"Self-employment tax" is my definition, since that is what seemed most often to be the determining factor. The Danish name for the tax is simply "business tax" (*erhvervsskat*), but even that does not account for the inclusion of titled personages. Since how the tax was assessed is unknown, it is difficult to come up with a completely comprehensive name.

Appendix 4.1: The Berling Family

Ernst Henrich Berling (1708–1750)
m. 1732—Cecile Høpfner (1716–1750)
(8 children—2 sons, died young; 2 daughters, married; 4 surviving sons—Johan Christian, Georg Christopher, Jørgen Mathias, Andreas Gotthard)

Johan Christian, printer (1733–1771)
m. 1767—Anne Marie Frick (1741–1807)
Johan Christian (1770–1826)

Georg Christopher, brewer and printer (1737–1778)
m. 1) 1766—Maria Catharina Godiche (1741–Feb. 2, 1772)
5 children, all died at birth; MC also died in childbirth, "was mother to 5 children, all of whom the Lord took at birth; but after the fifth birth she was called to God's rest."[1]

2) Oct. 9, 1772—Elisabeth Christine Godiche (1744–1801) [Maria Catharina's sister]
Ernst Andreas **Hartvig** (1775–1812), brewer and printer
Carl Christian (1776–1824) m.—Sophie **Hedevig** Glassing (1792–1859)
Johan **Carl** Ernst (1812–1871)[2] m. 1854—**Polly** Marie Knudine Haderup
Johanne Augusta (1814–1876)—m. Christen Hee Møller,

Jørgen Mathias (1741–1791), jeweler

Andreas Gotthard (1746–1781), declared incompetent

[names in bold are the ones by which people were known]

Appendix 4.2: Erich Erichsen (1752–1837)

Erich Erichsen was born in Odense, Denmark, in 1752. His father, Laurits, was a city mayor and part-owner of a sugar factory in Odense. At some point, Erich moved to Copenhagen and got a job with Christian Schaarup Black (or Blach). In 1784, eighteen months after Christian Schaarup died, his widow, Johanne, married the somewhat younger Erichsen. C.S.'s property was now probated and split between his widow, Johanne, and their two children. Johanne retained the business and the couple's house on Kongens Nytorv. Erichsen moved into the house and the business. He was incredibly successful in expanding the business, so, by the end of the century, Erichsen's company (still called C.S. Black's Widow & Co.) owned thirteen ships, the third largest shipping fleet in Denmark. Hard times during the Napoleonic Wars forced Erichsen to shift his focus to financial dealings, and the Danish state became one of his largest clients. Here, too, Erichsen was successful and managed to survive the Danish state's bankruptcy in 1813.

A devastating fire in Copenhagen in 1795 burnt down much of the city, including the Black/Erichsen house. Erichsen took the opportunity to build a huge, ostentatious new building (which is now the headquarters of *Den danske Bank*). While the house was being built, which coincided with the time of Johanne's death, Erichsen spent time in London, perhaps as long as two years. Although a member of *Grosserer-Societetet*'s three-man Executive Board at the time, his signature disappeared from their minutes. The common practice was to replace someone who had left, but Erichsen was not replaced. His signature reappeared years later, still as C.S. Black's Widow & Co. He was GS's chairman from 1817 until 1833. Erichsen eventually moved into his new mansion and lived there until his bankruptcy in 1833. In 1813, his brother Peter's widow, Anna Agate Appleby Erichsen, moved into the building with five of her six children and presumably acted as Erichsen's hostess for the rest of their stay.

When Erichsen was forced to declare bankruptcy in 1833, he owned, in addition to the house on Kongens Nytorv, a summer residence, Hellerupgaard, north of Copenhagen, several warehouses and a shipyard on Christianshavn, Whim Plantation on St. Croix in the Danish

West Indies, and several shipping vessels. He had been dealing in various financial matters for several years and was probably involved in the slave trade, although I have no proof of that. The folder containing the material that was submitted concerning his bankruptcy is several inches thick. It includes a letter from Erichsen, in which he says that he had hoped to be able to pay off all his creditors, but that, even after selling all his assets, he would be able to cover only 16 percent of his debts. The largest debt was apparently to Baring Brothers, merchants, in London. This was for 150,000 Danish *rigsdaler*, a sum so large I have no way to compare it to today's money. Baring Brothers were willing to accept Whim Plantation and the ship *Antoinette* as compensation for this debt, so long as Erichsen's other creditors agreed, which they did.

Erichsen was forced to sell the house on Kongens Nytorv and moved to a building on Skt. Annæ Plads, where he lived until his death. Skt. Annæ Øster, the district where Erichsen now lived, was quite exclusive. The building next door to the one in which Erichsen lived was occupied by Princess Louise Charlotte and her household. I have been unable to determine how much of the building on Skt. Annæ Plads Erichsen occupied. Did he have a floor, an apartment, a room? Was he a lodger with someone else, or was he able to maintain his own household?[3] In any case, although Erichsen was forced out of his luxurious home by his bankruptcy, he clearly did not slide all the way to the bottom of the social scale. The building he built on Kongens Nytorv still exists, and the second floor (first, European-style) retains room configurations and interior decorations much as it had been.[4]

Erichsen never remarried and had no known children. He brought two of his brother Peter's sons into the business with him. After the bankruptcy, these nephews moved to England, their mother's family's home, and successfully applied for English citizenship. The Erichsen family grave in Assistens Cemetery in Copenhagen was apparently taken over by the Sidoni family. Guiseppe Sidoni had married Hanne Erichsen, Peter's daughter and Erich's niece.

Sadly, there is very little left of what was an extraordinarily large fortune with corresponding influence.

Appendix 5.1: Job Titles of Married Women and Men (as given in business license application letters)

Wives

actor	9
auctioneer	1
author	2
baker	6
beer seller	1
boarding house host	4
butcher	1
candle seller	2
clothing seller	5
coffeeshop owner	1
distiller	2
engraver	1
firewood seller	1
fishmonger	1
graphic artist	1
greengrocer	10
innkeeper	3
junk dealer	17
landlord	1
leather dealer	2
market woman	8
meat dealer	3
midwife	49
military wife	640
painter	1
porter	1
probate evaluator	3
schoolkeeper	1
seamstress	17
seller	4
seller of imported goods	1
seller of old clothes	5
seller of thread and yarn	7
small shopkeeper	4
solo dancer	1
street stall seller	350
tobacco seller	1
watchmaker	1
weaver	2
wine merchant	1
women's clothing producer	27
women's clothing seller	2
wool or linen stocking seller	1

Husbands

actor	4
attendant or groundskeeper	1
author	1
blacksmith	1
brewer	1
buttonmaker	1
carpenter	2
colonel	1
cotton weaver	1
cutter	2

director of an institute	1
drummer	1
engraver	1
general lieutenant	1
goldsmith	2
gunner	3
hackney coach assistant	1
hatmaker	1
housepainter	1
infantryman	1
innkeeper, beer dispenser	4
journeyman builder	4
journeyman carpenter	2
journeyman goldsmith	1
journeyman housepainter	1
journeyman locksmith	1
journeyman shoemaker	1
journeyman silkweaver	1
journeyman tailor	1
journeyman tobacco spinner	1
journeyman, unspecified	2
landscape painter	1
language teacher	1
lawyer	1
lottery assistant	2
mat maker	1
merchant	1
musician	2
musketeer	2
naval gunner	1
naval mate	4
parish minister	1
pewterer	1
plasterer	1
porter	1
printer	1
professor	1
quartermaster	1
ropemaker	3
rye bread baker	1
saddlemaker	1
sailor	5
school teacher	1
sculptor	1
secretary	1
seller of East Indian goods	2
ship's captain	1
ship's carpenter	2
shoe repairer	1
shoemaker	6
skipper	12
small shopkeeper	1
soldier	1
sugar refiner	1
surgeon	1
tailor	8
teacher	1
ticket collector	1
unknown	63
waiter or servant	1
wheelwright	1
wigmaker	1
wine waiter	1
wool or linen clothier	4
worker	11

Notes

Chapter One

1. Louise A. Tilly and Joan W. Scott, *Women, Work, and Family* (New York: Holt, Rinehart and Winston, 1978); see especially chapter 3 for a discussion of "family economy."
2. Laurel Thatcher Ulrich, *Well-Behaved Women Seldom Make History* (New York: Alfred A. Knopf, 2007), "The Slogan," pp. xii–xxxiv. This sentence originally appeared in "Vertuous Women Found: New England Ministerial Literature, 1668–1735," *American Quarterly* 28, no. 1 (Spring 1976), p. 20.
3. Alice Clark, *Working Life of Women in the Seventeenth Century* (London: George Routledge & Sons, Ltd., 1919; repr., 1982, Routledge & Kegan Paul).
4. Joan W. Scott and Louise A. Tilly, "Women's Work and the Family in Nineteenth-Century Europe," in *The Economics of Women and Work*, ed. Alice H. Amsden (New York: St. Martin's Press, 1980), originally published in *Comparative Studies in Society and History* 17, no. 1 (Jan. 1975), pp. 36–64.
5. Tilly and Scott, *Women, Work, and Family.*
6. Inger Hartby, Kirsten Jexlev, Kirsten Rykind-Eriksen, and Anne Røssell, *Madammer og jomfruer—1700-tals kvinder i håndværk og handel* (Copenhagen: Nationalmuseet, 1986); "Handelsmadammer i 1700-tallet," *Siden Saxo* 4, no. 3 (1987), pp. 29-36. One could also challenge the assumption that women were ever "bound to the home," but that is another story.
7. Hannah Barker, *The Business of Women: Female Enterprise and Urban Development in Northern England, 1760-1830* (Oxford: Oxford University Press, 2006), pp. 2-3.
8. Nicola Phillips, *Women in Business, 1700-1850* (Woodbridge, Suffolk, UK: The Boydell Press, 2006), pp. 19–20.
9. Deborah Simonton and Anne Montenach, eds., *Female Agency in the Urban Economy: Gender in European Towns, 1640-1830* (New York and London: Routledge, 2013).
10. I invented the term "schoolkeeper" as a direct translation of the Danish *skoleholder.* It refers to people who owned and managed private, for-profit schools. The term was created to parallel similar terms such as innkeeper or shopkeeper, people who owned and ran their own businesses.

11. Carol Gold, *Educating Middle Class Daughters: Private Girls Schools in Copenhagen, 1790–1820* (Copenhagen: Museum Tusculanum Press, 1996), pp. 62–63.
12. *Stavnsbaandet,* which was in effect from 1733 to 1788, tied male peasants to their birth parish from age four to age forty. It never included women; the assumption was that where the men were, the women would stay.
13. Rasmus Nyerup, as quoted in Steffen Linvald, *I portenes skygge* (Copenhagen: Stig Vendelkærs Forlag, 1965), p. 9.
14. Sv. Cedergreen Bech, *Københavns Historie gennem 800 år* (Copenhagen: P. Haase & Søns Forlag, 1967), p. 376.
15. "Indkvarteringsmandtal," Copenhagen, Stadsarkivet, 1800-01.
16. Svend Aage Hansen, *Økonomisk vækst i Danmark* (Copenhagen: Universitetsforlag i København, G.E.C. Gads Forlag, 1972)}, vol. 1, p. 13.
17. One *kommercelæst* = 150 cubic feet or 2,600 kilograms.
18. Ole Feldbæk, *Danmarks økonomiske historie, 1500–1840* (Herning, Denmark: Systime, 1993), pp. 140 and 147.
19. Grosserer-Societetet, "Alfabetisk Register til Forhandlingsprotokol" (Århus, Denmark: Erhvervsarkivet, 1774–1790).
20. H.D. Schepelern, "Handel og Søfart i det 18. Aarhundrede," *København By og Erhverv gennem 500 Aar*, ed. Alfred Bindslev (Copenhagen: Forlaget Novografia, 1948).
21. Feldbæk, *Danmarks økonomiske historie*, p. 133; P.P. Sveistrup and Rich. Willerslev, *Den danske Sukkerhandels og Sukkerproduktions Historie* (Copenhagen: Institut for Historie og Samfundsøkonomi, Gyldendalske Boghandel, 1945), pp. 59–60, 75, 122.
22. Carol Gold, "The Danish Reform Era, 1784–1800" (Ph.D. dissertation, University of Wisconsin–Madison, 1975), pp. 176–87.
23. Schepelern, "Handel og Søfart."
24. Feldbæk, *Danmarks økonomiske historie*, p. 138.
25. Flemming Dahl, *Københavns Bystyre gennem 300 Aar*, vol. I—1648–1858 (Copenhagen: Ejnar Munksgaards Forlag, 1943), pp. 50, 51; Sv. Cedergreen Bech, *Storhandelens By* (Copenhagen: Gyldendal, 1981), pp. 94–99, says essentially the same thing.
26. 20 percent of the women picked up by the police in 1801 were charged either with illegal residency or with having no fixed abode

or occupation. Københavns Politimesteren. "Hovedjournal," nr. 13. Copenhagen, 1801.

27. *Kiøbenhavns kongelige allernaadigste privilegerede Adresse-Contoirs Efterretninger* (Copenhagen: Simmelkiærs Enke, 1791), p. 94.
28. Richard Willerslev, "Boligforholdene i København o. 1800," *Historiske Meddelelser om København* (1984).
29. *Adresseavisen* 33, no. 186 (Aug. 30, 1791).
30. Richard Willerslev, "Boligforhold og befolkningstruktur i København o. 1800," *Historiske Meddelelser om København* (1983).
31. K.H. Seidelin. *Politivennen* (Copenhagen: K.H. Seidelin, 1801).
32. The term *borger* or "citizen" changed meaning over the course of the nineteenth and twentieth centuries, from an earlier, premodern meaning of one who had the "freedom of the city," to a member of a nation state, frequently determined by the right to vote. Women received suffrage in Denmark in 1915.
33. Inger Dübeck, *Købekoner og konkurrence* (Copenhagen: Juristforbundets Forlag, 1978), p. 218. Supporting this interpretation is the fact that husbands did sometimes actively disapprove of or reject their wives' actions. There are several notices in *Adresseavisen* stating that a husband is no longer responsible for his wife's debts. In order for this to be possible, she would have had to have been able to contract the debt on her own in the first place.
34. Under the terms of the 1800 law regulating guilds, anyone born in the realm who had worked as a journeyman for four years could establish himself as a "free master" by paying half the appropriate guildmaster's entry fee. Guildmasters' fees varied depending on the specific guild. Carl Bruun, *Kjøbenhavn. En illustreret Skildring af dets Historie, Mindesmærker og Institutioner* (Copenhagen: Det nordiske Forlag, 1901), vol. 3, p. 863.
35. This concept still exists in Danish law and allows a surviving spouse to retain the family property, eliminating the necessity of dividing it with surviving children. All surviving children must still agree.
36. Christian Gottlob Prost, ed., *Veiviseren eller Anviisning til de flestes Boepæle i Kiøbenhavn og Forstæderne for Aaret 1801* (Copenhagen: Zacharius Bruun, 1801).
37. Heads of household were literally supposed to present themselves at pre-arranged centers to fill out the required questionnaires. Thomas

Munck, *The Enlightenment: A Comparative Social History 1721–1794* (London: Arnold, 2000), pp. 171–72.

38. Prior to the nineteenth century, the Danes used a font that they call "Gothic," which is very similar to the German "fraktur." The printed font has a handwritten form as well; most modern Danes can no longer decipher this handwriting.
39. It should be noted that scanned records retain the original "Gothic" printed font and as such are scanned in as pictures rather than as text; thus they are not electronically searchable.
40. Helle Linde claimed in an exhibition catalog that the king issued these licenses before 1800, but that the magistrate assumed this responsibility after 1800. I have found no evidence of such a chronological delineation; royal and communal licenses both span the 1800 divide. Grethe Ilsøe et al., *Søg—og I skal finde—Udstilling* (Copenhagen: Landsrkivet for Sjælland, 1991), p. 16.
41. Dahl, *Københvans Bystyre,* vol. I, pp. 36–37.
42. Københavns Magistrat, Raadstueskriveren, "Specification over Brændeviinsværkerne her udi den kongelige Residentz Stad Kiøbenhavn og Christianshavn," Copenhagen 1742.
43. Ibid. "Fortegnelse over dem, der har erholdt Bevilling til at handle med Østindiske og Vestindiske Varer," Copenhagen, ca. 1790.
44. Københavns Magistrat, 2. Sekretariat, "Protokol over Markedspasser," Copenhagen, 1775–1811. She did not have permission to sell leather goods or fine scarves. Usually this kind of an exclusion meant that the pass holder did not have access to approved guild goods.
45. Københavns Magistrat, 2. Hovedfag, "Journal." Copenhagen, Sept. 2, 1801–March 25, 1805, case no. 649.
46. Københavns Magistrat. 2. Sekretariat, "Cancelliet—yderlige Bestemmelse i andl. af visse Næringsvejes Tilladelse heri Staden," Copenhagen, 1817.
47. Gold, *Educating Middle Class Daughters.*
48. Københavns Magistrat, "Protokol over Markedspasser." This is a list of people who were given permission to travel from Copenhagen to markets. "Markedspasser, tilbageleverede," Copenhagen 1778–1826. These twenty-two boxes contain the actual returned passes, in alphabetical order by recipient's name.
49. Kjøbenvans Politiekammer, "General-Tabelle over Laugenes

Interessentere og Mestere, samt Svende og Drenge i Kjøbenhavn," (Copenhagen, 1806).

50. Københavns Raadstue, "Protokol over samtlige til Staden henhørende og under Magistraten værende Betieninger," Copenhagen 1739–1805.
51. A *matrikel* number is a house number that is unique to a district, rather than to a street. So houses are numbered up and down streets throughout the district, with no repetitions within the district.
52. Raadstueskriveren [Johan Thomas Flindt], "Tegne-Bog vedkommende Kiøbenhavns borgerlige Væsen forfattet Ao. 1794 October Maaned af J. Th. F.," Copenhagen, 1794. This has a very detailed account of the city's finances, which I found absolutely opaque and completely incomprehensible. It is also worth noting that the metric system was not yet in use; money was based on a six scale (1 *rigsdaler* = 6 *mark* = 96 *skilling*).
53. Politimesteren, "Hovedjournal," no. 13 (1801).
54. [J. Th. F.], "Tegne-Bog vedkommende Kiøbenhavns borgerlige Væsen."
55. Københavns Raadstue, "Protokol over samtlige til Staden henhørende og under Magistraten værende Betieninger."

Chapter Two

1. Københavns Magistrat, 2. sekretariat, "Markedspasser, tilbageleverede," Copenhagen, 1778–1826; "Folketælling," Copenhagen, 1801.
2. Københavns Magistrat, 2. sekretariat, "Ansøgninger om Stadesedler for Gadehandel med Brød, Frugt, o.l." (nos. 431–778), Copenhagen, 1807–1816, no. 725/1816. By "work," she meant working for someone else, primarily as a servant, or as a member of someone else's household.
3. Ibid., nos. 654–62/1816. Unfortunately, I have no information on when Caspar died, how old either he or his widow was, nor how long she continued to run the bakery after his death. Dorothea is, however, listed as paying self-employment taxes in 1801, which is fifteen years earlier. At some point, her son, Phillip Daniel, joined her in the business.

4. Richard Willerslev, "Boligforholdene i København o. 1800," *Historiske Meddelelser om København* (1984).
5. K.H. Seidelin, "Politivennen" (Copenhagen: K.H. Seidelin, 1801), no. 142 (Jan. 10, 1801), pp. 2271–72. Emphasis in original.
6. Ibid., no. 143 (Jan. 17, 1801), 2286–87.
7. "Ansøgninger om Stadesedler for Gadehandel med Brød, Frugt, o.l." (nos. 431–778). Case no. 725.
8. See Natalie Zemon Davis, *Fiction in the Archives: Pardon Tales and the Tellers in Sixteenth-Century France* (Stanford, CA: Stanford University Press, 1987), for a discussion of boilerplate applications.
9. "Ansøgninger om Stadesedler for Gadehandel med Brød, Frugt, o.l." (nos. 431–778). No. 708/1816.
10. Ibid., no. 755/1816.
11. Ibid., no. 447/1807.
12. Ibid. See, for example, nos. 437 and 654–662.
13. Københavns Magistrat, "Protocoll over udstedte Sælgesedler til dem som gaae omkring paa Gaden og sælge Fisk, etc." 1773–1819.
14. Københavns Magistrat, 2. sekretariat, "Deponerede og kasserede kongelige Næringsbevillinger," Copenhagen, 1779–1834.
15. It has been suggested, although without any proof, that peddling yarn and ribbons may have been a cover for prostitution.
16. Københavns Politimesteren, "Hovedjournal," no. 13, Copenhagen, 1801.
17. C. Klug-Andersen, "Torvehandelen," *København By og Erhverv gennem 500 Aar*, ed. Alfred Bindslev (Copenhagen: Forlaget Novografia, 1948), p. 396; Steffen Linvald, *I portenes skygge* (Copenhagen: Stig Vendelkærs Forlag, 1965), pp. 80–81.
18. Københavns Magistrat, 2. sekretariat, "Protokol over Markedspasser," Copenhagen, 1775–1811.
19. "Markedspasser, tilbageleverede."
20. The discrepancy between the number of returned passes (68) and the total number given here (103) reflects the fact that I included women I found elsewhere who traveled to markets.
21. There are 121 passes on this list, rather than 103, because when women were given permission to sell different sorts of goods, I listed it twice. I was more interested in the kinds of goods sold than in the actual number of women, which can not be accurately known, in any case.

22. "Protokol over Markedspasser."
23. Ibid.
24. Ibid.; "Markedspasser, tilbageleverede."
25. "Indkvarteringsmandtal," Copenhagen: Stadsarkivet, 1771. It was not uncommon for independent or master craftsmen to own their own buildings. Typically, they would have a shop on the ground floor, live in back and/or on the first floor (second floor, American style), and then rent out rooms, apartments, or space in the rest of the building. The property sometimes also included a side or back building. There are numerous ads for this sort of space to rent in *Adresseavisen*. Richard Willerslev estimates that in 1801 there were an average of 26–27 people per building in Copenhagen. Slightly over half the apartments had only one or two rooms. Willerslev, "Boligforholdene i København."
26. "Markedspasser, tilbageleverede"; Helle Linde, "Modehandel og kasketsalg—kvinder som selvstændige næringsdrivende i København 1845," in *Søg–og I skal finde*, eds. Grethe Ilsøe, Karen Hjorth, and Birgitte Possing (Copenhagen: ARKI.Varia, 1991).
27. "Indkvarteringsmandtal," 1771; "Indkvarteringsmandtal," 1800–01.

Chapter Three

1. Københavns Magistrat, 2. sekretariat, "Deponerede og kasserede kommunale Bevillinger," Copenhagen 1779–1857. License date, Sept. 24, 1821.
2. "Ansøgninger om Stadesedler for Gadehandel med Brød, Frugt, o.l.," Copenhagen, March 10, 1815, nos. 654–662; "Folketælling," Copenhagen, 1787 and 1801.
3. "Deponerede og kasserede kommunale Bevillinger," original license, Oct. 2, 1822.
4. See Rebecca L. Spang, *The Invention of the Restaurant—Paris and Modern Gastronomic Culture* (Cambridge, MA, and London: Harvard University Press, 2000), for a discussion of the distinction between "restaurants" and earlier forms of eating establishments.

    See Amanda Vickery, *Behind Closed Doors: At Home in Georgian England* (New Haven, CT, and London: Yale University Press, 2009), chapter 2, "Men Alone," for a discussion of the eating and sleeping arrangements of single men in early modern London. Although Vickery concentrates on single men, at least in Copenhagen there were also women on their own in the city. Several advertisements in *Adresseavisen* are directed towards women. "A respectable woman who requires board and lodging can receive this at Studiestræde no. 63, on the third floor" (June 27, 1791, no. 137), or "A respectable woman or man can have room and board, etc., starting at Michaelmas, in a respectable house on Gothersgade, no. 5, third floor, just off Kongens Nytorv" (Aug. 23, 1791, no. 181).

5. [Ernst Christian] Hauberg, *Kiøbenhavns kongelige Adresse-Contoirs Efterretninger* (Copenhagen: Morthorskee Enke & Comp. (?), 1801), Jan. 2, 1801, no. 1.
6. As an odd footnote to the institution of such sweet shops, on July 29, 1815 the Copenhagen Board of Education sent a circular to all schools in the city stating that it was illegal for innkeepers, confectioners, and restaurant owners to sell to children. The rationale given was that sweets were not good for children, but there was also an unacknowledged concern about unsupervised children in such places. Carol Gold, *Educating Middle Class Daughters: Private Girls Schools in Copenhagen, 1790–1820* (Copenhagen: Museum Tusculanum Press, 1996), p. 75.
7. Københavns Magistrat, 2. sekretariat, "Deponerede og kasserede kongelige Næringsbevillinger," Copenhagen 1779–1834.
8. "Deponerede og kasserede kommunale Bevillinger."
9. Ibid.
10. See licenses for Bolette Cathrine Dein (1834), Ane Margrethe Elmqvist (1835), Frederikke Catherine Hansen (1834), Anne Iversen (1833), Mrs. Ole Larsen (1835), and Beate Antinette Møller (1821). Ibid.
11. Wolfgang Schivelbusch, *Tastes of Paradise: A Social History of Spices, Stimulants, and Intoxicants* (New York: Vintage, 1992) pp. 34, 52.
12. *Ordbog over det danske Sprog.* http://ordnet.dk/ods/ordbog?query=almue.
13. Københavns Raadstue, "Protokol over samtlige til Staden henhørende og under Magistraten værende Betieninger," Copenhagen, 1739–1805. See also Københavns Stadsarkiv, "Register til Stadens Betjeninger i det 18. Aarhundrede. Fortegnelse over Bryggere, hvis Svende har aflagt Ed paa Raadstuen 1755–1805" (Copenhagen). This

register refers to the previous "Protokol" but just lists brewers. Out of a total of 350 guild brewers in the city between 1755 and 1805, forty-eight were women.

14. Raadstueskriveren, "Specification over Brændeviinsværkerne her udi den kongelige Residentz Stad Kiøbenhavn og Christianshavn," Copenhagen, 1742.
15. "Genpart af Privilegier," Copenhagen, 1692–1772.
16. Ibid.
17. Københavns Magistrat, 2. Hovedfag, "Journal." Copenhagen, Sept. 2, 1801–March 25, 1805. License August 23, 1804.
18. "Indkvarteringsmandtal," Copenhagen, Stadsarkivet, 1800–01.
19. Harald Ilsøe, *Bogtrykkerne i København og deres virksomhed ca. 1600–1810* (Copenhagen: Det Kongelige Bibliotek and Museum Tusculanums Forlag, 1992).
20. Ibid. "Indkvarteringsmandtal," 1801.
21. Københavns Magistrat, "Deponerede og kasserede kommunale Bevillinger."
22. Københavns Magistrat, 2. Hovedfag, "Kopibog," Copenhagen, 1801–1805, no. 132.
23. Rebslagerlavet, "Protocoll," Copenhagen, Københavns Stadsarkiv, 1773–1864; "Folketælling," 1787 and 1801.
24. Københavns Magistrat, 2. sekretariat, "Protokol over Markedspasser," Copenhagen, 1775–1811; Copenhagen, "Indkvarteringsmandtal," 1771 and 1801; Rebslagerlavet, "Protocoll"; Politimesteren, "Hovedjournal," no. 13 (1801), items #4126 and 4229.
25. "Genpart af Privilegier," no. 388.
26. Københavns Kommune, "Borgerskabs Protocol, fra den 2. Januar 1805 til den 28. Decb 1819."
27. Deborah Simonton, *A History of European Women's Work: 1700 to the Present* (London: Routledge, 1998), p. 80.
28. The President, Mayors and Council,
In the royal residence city of Copenhagen,
Make known: that, as

[*applicant's name*] ________________________________
lives separated from her husband

[*husband's name*] ______________________________
has applied for permission to continue in the same civil occupation of

[*business*] ______________________________, for which he on the

[*date*] ____________________ received citizenship here in the city; so we have, in accordance with the Royal Danish Chancellery's resolution of September 23, 1798, so that such divorced wives, in order not to become a burden for society, may enjoy the same rights as widows, when they bear the same burdens, we grant that she, as long as she does not enter into another marriage, may here in the city continue the aforementioned commonly held occupation

[*business*], ______________________________
though she shall be bound to pay the same civil occupational tax, the same as others who carry out the same trade here in the city. Københavns Raadstue, "Betieninger."

29. Gordon Norrie, *Det Danske Jordemodervæsens Historie*, *Danmarks Jordemødre*, ed. W. Nellemose (Copenhagen: Dansk Medicinsk-historisk Selskab, 1935), p. 55.
30. Ibid., pp. 35–36. Interestingly, in 1783 the Midwife Commission decided that specifically Jewish midwives were not necessary; Jewish women could use Christian midwives, the Commission reasoned. One wonders how often they did in actuality; p. 54.
31. Københavns Raadstue, "Betieninger."
32. *Kiøbenhavns kongelig allernaadigst privilergerede Adresse-Contoirs Efterretninger* (Copenhagen: Simmelkiærs Enke, 1791), pp. 35 and 92.
33. According to a law of January 1, 1861, "people who have had accidents on the street or suddenly become sick must be taken in by any barber shop in Copenhagen, and the barber shall offer them what temporary and immediate help he thinks necessary and comfortable to offer." *Ordbog over det danske Sprog*, http://ordnet.dk/ods/ordbog?aselect=Barber&query=barbere.
34. Københavns Magistrat, "Journal," 1802, nos. 860, 986, and 1122.
35. Langkilde lists seventeen women whose licenses date from before 1740. However, Langkilde's catalog does not include all the women

schoolkeepers. I found almost twice as many as he did for the period between 1790 and 1820. Hans P. Langkilde, "Langkildes Skolekartotek," Copenhagen: Stadsarkivet, 1946 (?); Gold, *Educating Middle Class Daughters.*

36. Gold, *Educating Middle Class Daughters*, pp. 60–62.
37. Ibid., p. 62.
38. See, for example, letter of Sept. 12, 1833, from Caroline Henckel, asking for money from Erich Erichsen's bankruptcy proceedings to tide her over while her husband, Christian Frederick Henckel, was at sea. Henckel was a petty officer on the *Antoinette,* a ship owned by Erichsen, but Erichsen went bankrupt in 1833. There is a longer discussion of this in the next chapter. "Arrangements- og Liquidations-Commissionen i Handelshuset Black Enke & Co. [Erichsen Bankruptcy Papers]," *Eksekutorboer, 1790–1919* (Copenhagen: Rigsarkivet, 1833).
39. Nicolai Edinger Balle, "Efterretninger om Kirke-, Fattige- og Friskoler i København, indsendte i henhold til Danske Kancellis Cirkulære 1790, 10. Juli," in Danske Kancelli, Kommission angaaende det almindelige Skolevæsen, 5a. Diverse. Copenhagen, Rigsarkivet, 1791. Nothing more is said of Mr. Ernst, so we do not know of what the "disorder" consisted.

    For more on female schoolkeepers, see the section on Anette Linde in the next chapter and in my book on girls schools. Gold, *Educating Middle Class Daughters.*
40. Olwen Hufton, *The Prospect before Her: A History of Women in Western Europe, 1500–1800*, vol. 1 (New York: Alfred A. Knopf, 1996), p. 174.

Chapter Four

1. "Indkvarteringsmandtal," Copenhagen, Stadsarkivet, 1771; "Indkvarteringsmandtal," Copenhagen, Stadsarkivet, 1801.
2. "Indkvarteringsmandtal," 1801. There are discrepancies in the numbers of women who paid this tax. This is because I was interested in occupations, not in total absolute numbers, which I figured would never be completely accurate in any case. So, although a total of 458 women were listed in the 1801 tax register, I recorded only 240 in

my database. Of the remaining 218, 15 were listed by their husbands' government titles (Mrs. State Counsellor), 78 were landlords, and the remaining 125 had no listed occupation or title.

3. *Berlingske Tidende* (The Berling Times) still exists as a daily newspaper in Copenhagen. www.b.dk.
4. Bent Blünikow, "Ernst Henrich Berling og hans fingeraftryk," *Berlingske Tidende*, March 21, 2008.
5. Harald Ilsøe, *Bogtrykkerne i København og deres virksomhed ca. 1600–1810* (Copenhagen: Det Kongelige Bibliotek and Museum Tusculanums Forlag, 1992), p. 226.
6. "Indkvarteringsmandtal," 1801.
7. T. Vogel-Jørgensen, *Berlingske Tidende gennem to hundrede Aar, 1749–1949* (Copenhagen: Det Berlingske Bogtrykkeri, 1949), vol. I, p. 180.
8. Although there is a genealogical tree in Vogel-Jørgensen, *Berlingske Tidende,* many of the family relationships have also been pieced together from a collection of printed (but not published) songs that are available in the Royal Library. [J.E. Glasing], ed., *Lejlighedsdigte fra den Berlingske Familie*, 2 vols. (Copenhagen: unpublished, 1750–1808).
9. Københavns Skiftekommission Hof- og Stadsretten, "Samfrænde Brev, Georg Christopher Berling," in *Bevillinger og Samfrændeskiftebreve* (Copenhagen: Rigsarkivet, 1778), box 3, no 28/1778.
10. Johan Carl Ernst Berling, "Materiale vedr. Bladet og Trykkeriet," Copenhagen: Rigsarkivet, 1748–1869, F.8. Diverse vedr. *Berlingske Tidende*, 1788–1862.
11. Vogel-Jørgensen., *Berlingske Tidende,* vol. I, p. 144.
12. Ibid., vol. I, p. 145.
13. Ibid.
14. Københavns Kommune, "[Vurderinger over det Berlingske Hus]," in *Syns- og taksationsforretninger over fast ejendom [Vurderinger]* (Copenhagen: Stadsarkivet, 1712–1964), Købmager kvarter, matrikel nr. 118.
15. "Borgerskabs Protokol," Copenhagen, 1749–1784; Københavns Politimesteren, "Hovedjournal, Nr. 13," Copenhagen, 1801, nr. 2309; "Bryggerikommissionens Protokol—Københavns Politi. udtagne

Sager C." Copenhagen: Landsarkivet for Sjælland m.m. [now in Rigsarkivet, Copenhagen], 1795–1805.

16. T. Vogel-Jørgensen, "Da Flyttelæssene arriverede i Pilestræde 3. April 1765," *Berlingske Tidende,* 1930, p. 14.
17. "Indkvarteringsmandtal," 1764, 1766, 1771, 1778, 1801, 1806, 1811.
18. *Lejlighedsdigte fra den Berlingske Familie.*
19. "Indkvarteringsmandtal," 1801; Christian Gottlob Prost, ed., *Veiviseren eller Anviisning til de flestes Boepæle i Kiøbenhavn og Forstæderne for Aaret 1801* (Copenhagen: Zacharius Bruun, 1801).
20. Ilsøe, *Bogtrykkerne i København,* p. 5.
21. Vogel-Jørgensen, *Berlingske Tidende gennem to hundrede Aar,* vol. I, p. 146; Ilsøe, *Bogtrykkerne i København,* p. 5; Vogel-Jørgensen disagrees that E.C. Berling ran the company (p. 141), although he gives no proof for his assertion that she did not.
22. Københavns Kommune, Købmager kvarter, matrikel nr. 118. *Syns- og taksationsforretninger over fast ejendom.*
23. Københavns Skiftekommission Hof- og Stadsretten, "Samfrænde Brev, Philibert Bonfils," *Bevillinger og samfrændeskiftebreve* (Copenhagen: Rigsarkivet, 1771–1775), box 1, no. 8/1773.
24. Københavns Skiftekommission Hof- og Stadsretten, "[Henrich Bonfils' Bankruptcy Papers, 1788]," *Forseglings Protokol* (Copenhagen: Rigsarkivet, 1780–1785), 6B, pp. 241–244; "[Henrich Bonfils's Probate Records]," *Forseglings Protokol* (Copenhagen: Rigsarkivet, 1771–1797), 4D, pp. 72–77.
25. Københavns Skiftekommission Hof- og Stadsretten, "Samfrændebrev, P. Bonfils," *Bevillinger og samfrændeskiftebrev* (Copenhagen: Rigsarkivet, 1788), box 15, 16/1788.
26. "Bryggerikommissionens Protokol," Aug. 28, 1798.
27. "Indkvarteringsmandtal," 1763, 1764, 1771, 1778, 1795, 1801.
28. Jens Vibæk, *Reform og Fallit, 1784–1830* (Copenhagen: Politiken, 1964).
29. Vilh. Lorenzen, ed., *Grosserer-Societetet 1742–1942* (Copenhagen: Gyldendal, 1942), p. 68.
30. Grosserer-Societetet, "Forhandlingsprotokol" (Århus, Denmark: Erhvervsarkivet, 1774–90), pp. 19–23.
31. It is hard to sort out the difference between "skippers" and "captains." While "captains" were always in charge, it need not be on a

ship. One could be a captain in the miltia. "Skippers," on the other hand, always worked on ships, but an older meaning of the word also translates to "sailor," as in "one who ships." "Agent" was as much a title as an occupation. Erich Erichsen, Johanne Wadum's second husband, is often listed in records as "Agent Erichsen." About four hundred people are listed as "landlords," so passive income was included.

32. A riotous send-up of *Adresseavisen* can be found in [anonymous], "Skilderie af vore Tider," *Et original Ugeblad* (Copenhagen, 1790–91), nr. 14 (April 1, 1791). Note the date; it's an April Fool's joke.
33. *Kiøbenhavns kongelig Adresse-Contoirs Efterretninger* (Copenhagen: Morthorskee Enke & Comp. (?), 1801), Jan. 9, 1801, nr. 11.
34. Ibid., 1791, nr. 8; *Berlingske Tidende*, Dec. 20, 1790.
35. Specifically, Isaac Benners was married to Nancy Applebye Erichsen's sister, Marie Christine Applebye. Nancy was Peter Erichsen's wife and Erich Erichsen's hostess after his brother Peter died. When Isaac Benners first came to Copenhagen from the West Indies, he was accompanied by one of his slaves, Peter Samuel.
36. Københavns Skiftekommission Hof- og Stadsretten, "Samfrænde Brev, C.S. Black," *Bevillinger og samfrændeskiftebreve* (Copehagen: Rigsarkivet, 1783).
37. [Københavns Magistrat], "Prioritetsvurderinger," in *Syns- og taksationsforretninger over faste ejendom* (Copenhagen: Stadsarkivet), Øster kv. nr 264; Hans Helge Madsen, *Interiørdekorationer i Erichsens Palæ—fra arkitekten J.J. Ramés virke i København* (Copenhagen: Aktieselskabet Kjøbenhavns Handelsbank, 1968).
38. Lorenzen, ed., *Grosserer-Societetet*, pp. 138–39, 165, 147–48; Johannes Werner, *Christian Wilhelm Duntzfelt, En Dansk Storkøbmand fra den glimrende Handelsperiode, Skildringer* (Copenhagen, 1927), p. 41; Harald Jørgensen, "Erich Erichsen," *Dansk Biografisk Leksikon*, ed. Sv. Cedergreen Bech (Copenhagen: Gyldendal, 1980).
39. Lorenzen, ed., *Grosserer-Societetet.* Daniel Rabuzzi repeats the assertion, stating that Wadum "clearly played a subordinate role despite lending her name to the enterprise," but his only sources are earlier historians. Daniel A. Rabuzzi, "Fading Images, Fading Realities? Female Merchants in Scandinavia and the Baltic," *Social History/ Histoire Sociale* 34, no. 68 (2001), p. 359.

40. By comparison, the Berling widows, who inherited their husbands' firm in 1788, continued to use their husbands' name—Brødrene Berling (The Brothers Berling).
41. One is tempted to construct an entire novel around this couple. Johanne's first husband, C.S., was twelve years older than she was. Did she want to get married? Was this a marriage of convenience between two successful middle-class families? Or was Johanne encouraged by her parents to "marry up"? Erichsen, on the other hand, was three years younger than Johanne—a modern man who signed his name with confidence and no unnecessary flourishes and did not wear a wig, at least not in his later portrait. Maybe the two fell in love while he was working for her first husband? After her death, Erichsen never remarried, despite the fact that he was probably one of the wealthiest men in Copenhagen and not bad looking!
42. Carol Gold, *Educating Middle Class Daughters* (Copenhagen: Museum Tusculanum Press, 1996).
43. The 1787 census lists a Severine Holm married to merchant Marius Gotthard Holm. She was probably Franz Hinr. Kreutzfeld's widow since there were two children, Johan Severin Kreutzfeld and Hinriette Jacobine Kreutzfeldt, both listed as children of the wife's first marriage. The ages are possible, and it would not have been uncommon for Severine to marry someone from the same background.
44. Grosserer-Societetet, "Journalsager" (Århus, Denmark: Erhvervsarkivet, 1795–97).
45. Grosserer- Societetet, "Journalsager" (Århus: Erhvervsarkivet, 1781–90, 1792–94). Oddly, the "E"s are different. Erichsen seems to use one form of the capital E when signing as C.S. Blacks Enke (Widow), and a different form when signing his own name.
46. Skt. Nikolaj sogn, *Kirkebog,* 1800. "Q80," www.danishfamilysearch.dk/sogn659/churchbook/source136098/opslag14771450.
47. Maria Ekberger, "Andreas Bodenhoff: Leverandør til søetaten i det 18. århundrede," *Maritim Kontakt* 13 (1989), pp. 36–37. Bodenhoff's firm was eventually inherited by his daughter-in-law, Giertrud Birgitte Bodenhoff, another woman business owner. However, she ran the firm for only two years, from 1796 to 1798, before dying at the age of twenty. Nanna Lange, *Den Bodenhoffske Slægtebog* (Copenhagen: A. Rosenbergs Bogtrykkeri, 1914).

48. "Indkvarteringsmandtal," 1771; [Københavns Magistrat], "Prioritetsvurderinger," Øster kv. 154.
49. Jul. Schovelin, *Fra den Danske Handels Empire—Forhold og Personer i det 18. Aarhundredes sidste Halvdel* (Copenhagen: Det Nordiske Forlag, 1899), vol. 1, p. 151.
50. Rabuzzi. "Fading Images, Fading Realities?" pp. 359–60; Eiler Nystrøm, "Henning Frederik Bargum," *Dansk Biografisk Leksikon*, ed. Sv. Cedergreen Bech (Copenhagen: Gyldendal, 1980), v. 1, p. 455.
51. [Københavns Magistrat], *Prioritetsvurderinger.* Øster kv. 154.
52. Kaj Foltmar, "Frøken Frederica Louise Ernst, Fabrikant og Negotiant i Københavns florissante Handelstid," *Historiske Meddelelser om København* (1966).
53. Ibid., p. 100.
54. Ibid., p. 104.
55. Peter Edelberg, "De ældste led af slægten Fenger" (Copenhagen, 2006 [?]), p. 8. Author's private collection.
56. Ibid.
57. Nicolai Jonathan Meinert, "Københavnerliv ombring 1800—Grosserer Nicolai Jonathan Meinerts erindringer ved redaktionen," *Historiske Meddelelser om København* (1970), p. 86.
58. Ibid.
59. Edelberg, "De ældste led af slægten Fenger," p. 10.
60. Carol Gold, *Educating Middle Class Daughters.*
61. "Folketælling," Copenhagen 1787. The 1787 census lists one Linde as a goldsmith; this was Lorents, whose wife, aged 24, was Agnette (which could easily be a misspelling of Anette). The couple had no children. The oldest daughter, Vilhelmine Charlotte, would be born the following year.
62. Gold, *Educating Middle Class Daughters,* pp. 68–69; Gold, "Copenhagen Schoolkeepers" (Copenhagen City Archives, 1996), ref. no. 162.
63. Gold, *Educating Middle Class Daughters,* p. 143.
64. Direktionen for Almue- og Borgerskolevæsenet i København. 1815/205 and 1821/60; http://starbas.dk/pdf/schoolkeepers_database.pdf. #86.

Chapter Five

1. M. Sibbern, *Kiøbenhavnsbladet eller Borgeren og Politiet* (Copenhagen, C.F. Holm Enke), "Pigeskoler," Apr. 10, 1806, no. 181, p. 2951. Emphasis added.
2. Ibid., p. 2946.
3. Gold, *Educating Middle Class Daughters,* pp. 18, 81–99, and 41–52.
4. Københavns Magistrat, 2. sekretariat, "Deponerede og kasserede kommunale Bevillinger," Copenhagen, 1826.
5. Københavns Magistrat, "Deponerede og kasserede kongelige Næringsbevillinger," Copenhagen, 1820.
6. Københavns Magistrat, 2. Hovedfag, "Journal" (Copenhagen, Stadsarkivet) 1803, no. 430; "Kopibog," 1803, nr. 154.
7. Københavns Magistrat, 2. Hovedfag, "Deponerede og kasserede kongelige Næringsbevillinger."
8. Ibid.
9. Københavns Magistrat, "Journal," 1801, nr. 16.
10. Københavns Magistrat, "Deponerede og kasserede kommunale bevillinger."
11. Københavns Magistrat, "Deponerede og kasserede kongelige Næringsbevillinger."
12. Ibid.; "Indkvarteringsmandtal," 1811.
13. Københavns Magistrat, "Deponerede og kasserede kommunale bevillinger," 1801.
14. Ibid.

Appendices

1. [J.E. Glasing], ed., *Lejlighedsdigte fra den Berlingske Familie,* Copenhagen, unpublished, 1750–1808.
2. There is a coda to this story. Carl Berling (Johan Carl Ernst, who was Elisabeth Christine's grandson) and Louise Rasmussen were long-time lovers and had a son in 1840, Carl Christian Jacobsen. Louise later (in 1850) married King Frederik VII "to the left hand" and was given the title of Countess Danner. Carl's mother and sister objected vociferously to Carl's relationship with Louise, whom they viewed as a not quite proper woman, but the relation-

ship continued throughout their lives, including after her marriage to Frederik. Bodil Wamberg, *Grevinde—et portræt af Grevinde Danner* (Copenhagen: Bogklubben, 2005).

3. Serendipitously, the 1834 census from Skt. Annæ Øster has survived, although most of that year's census is missing, but Erichsen had not yet moved when the census was taken in February. By the time of the next census, he was dead, so, although I know his street address from the city directories, I have no idea how much of the address he occupied. According to the 1834 census, there were forty-four people living in number 11, Skt. Annæ Plads.
4. Hans Helge Madson, *Interiørdekorationer i Erichsens Palæ—Fra arkitekten J.J. Ramés virke i København* (Copenhagen: Aktieselskabet Kjøbenhavns Handelsbank, 1968).

Bibliography

Primary Sources

Archival

Copenhagen City Archives [Stadsarkivet], Copenhagen, Denmark

Dahl, Flemming. "Register til Borgerskabsprotokol, 1805–1806." Copenhagen: Stadsarkivet, 1934.

[Flindt, Johan Thomas, Borgermester]. Raadstueskriveren. "Tegne-Bog vedkommende Kiøbenhavns borgerlige Væsen forfattet Ao. 1794 October Maaned af J. Th. F." Copenhagen: Stadsarkivet, 1794.

"Folketælling." Copenhagen: Stadsarkivet, 1787, 1801.

"Genpart af Privilegier." Copenhagen: Stadsarkivet, 1692–1772.

Indqvarterings Commission. *Indqvarterings Commissionens Protocol.* Copenhagen: Stadsarkivet, 1760–1798.

"Indkvarteringsmandtal." Copenhagen: Stadsarkivet, 1771, 1801, 1811.

Københavns Kommune. "Borgerskabs Protocol, fra den 2. Januar 1805 til den 28. Decb 1819." Copenhagen: Stadsarkivet.

———. "Borgerskabs Protokol, 1749–1784." Copenhagen: Stadsarkivet.

———. "Borgerskabs Register, 1785–1795." Copenhagen: Stadsarkivet, 1943.

Københavns Magistrat. "Marskandisere—ubevilligede Ansøgninger." Copenhagen: Stadsarkivet, 1742–43.

———. "Prioritetsvurderinger." Syns- og taksationsforretninger over faste ejendom. Copenhagen: Stadsarkivet, 1712–1964.

———. "Protocoll over udstedte Sælgesedler til dem som gaae omkring paa Gaden og sælge Fisk, etc."

Københavns Magistrat, 2. Hovedfag. "Journal." Copenhagen: Stadsarkivet, 1801–1805.

———. "Journalsager." Copenhagen: Stadsarkivet, 1801–1805.

———. "Kopibog." Copenhagen: Stadsarkivet, 1801–1805.

Københavns Magistrat, 2. Sekretariat. "Ansøgninger om Stadesedler for Gadehandel med Brød, Frugt, o.l. (nos. 431 – 778)." Copenhagen: Stadsarkivet, 1807–1816.

———. "Cancelliet…Bestemmelser i andl. af visse Næringsvejes Tilladelse heri Staden." Copenhagen: Stadsarkivet, 1817.

———. "Deponerede og kasserede kommunale Bevillinger." Copenhagen: Stadsarkivet, 1779–1857, 1801.
———. "Deponerede og kasserede kongelige Næringsbevillinger." Copenhagen: Stadsarkivet, 1779–1834.
———. "Markedspasser, tilbageleverede." Copenhagen: Stadsarkivet, 1778–1826.
———. "Navneregister til kasserede og deponderede kommunale Bevillinger og kongelige Bevillinger." Copenhagen: Stadsarkivet, 1770–1857.
———. "Protokol over Markedspasser." Copenhagen: Stadsarkivet, 1775–1811.
Kjøbenhavns Politiekammer. "General-Tabelle over Laugenes Interessentere og Mestere, samt Svende og Drenge i Kjøbenhavn." Copenhagen: Stadsarkivet, 1806.
København Raadstue. "Extract af Grund-Taxtens Matricul over de Huuse og Gaarde i Kiøbenhavn og Christianshavn, som er taxerit i Grund Taxt for 300 Rdl. og derover,…" Copenhagen: Stadsarkivet, 1742 (?).
———. "Fortegnelse over dem, der har erholdt Bevilling til at handle med østindiske og vestindiske Varer." Copenhagen: Stadsarkivet, 1790.
———. "Fortegnelse over dem, der har faaet Bevilling til at være Marskandisere." Copenhagen: Stadsarkivet, 1797–1814.
———. "Laugssager vedr. Brændevinsbrænderne." Copenhagen: Stadsarkivet, 1761–1797.
———. "Kiøbenhavns Raadstue Protocoll." Copenhagen: Stadsarkivet, 1785–1795.
———. "Kiøbenhavns Raadstue-Protocoll, 1795–1804." Copenhagen: Stadsarkivet, 1804.
———. "Protokol over samtlige til Staden henhørende og under Magistraten værende Betieninger." Copenhagen: Stadsarkivet, 1739–1805.
———. "Specification over Brændeviinsværkerne her udi den kongelige Residentz Stad Kiøbenhavn og Christianshavn." Copenhagen: Stadsarkivet, 1742.
Københavns Stadsarkiv. "Alfabetisk Fortegnelse over Kommunale Bestillingsmænd, 1700–1857." Copenhagen: Stadsarkivet.
———. "Register til Stadens Betjeninger i det 18. Aarhundrede.

———. Fortegnelse over Bryggere, hvis Svende har aflagt Ed paa Raadstuen 1755–1805." Copenhagen: Stadsarkivet.
Langkilde, Hans P. "Langkildes Skolekartotek." Copenhagen: Stadsarkivet, 1946 (?).
Linvald, Axel. "Register til Borgerskabsprotokol 11. Maj 1795–31. December 1804." Copenhagen: Stadsarkivet, 1934.
Rasmussen, Ester. "Register til 'Bøger' No. 24. Privilegier 1696–1772." Copenhagen: Stadsarkivet, 1971.
Rebslagerlavet. "Protocoll." Copenhagen: Stadsarkivet, 1773–1864.

Sjælland, Lolland-Falster and Bornholm Provincial Archives [Landsarkivet for Sjælland, Lolland-Falster og Bornholm] (now combined with the Danish National Archives) [Rigsarkivet], Copenhagen, Denmark

Jørgensen, Harald. "Københavnske Politi- og Domsmyndigheder: Foreløbige arkivregistraturer." Copenhagen: Landsarkivet for Sjælland, m.m. 1975.
Københavns Politi. "Bryggerikommissionens Protokol." Copenhagen: Landsarkivet for Sjælland. m.m., 1795–1805.
Københavns Politimesteren. "Hovedjournal, Nr. 13." Copenhagen: Landsarkivet for Sjælland, m.m., 1801.
Københavns Politiret. "Sageliste ved 1. Protocoll." Copenhagen: Landsarkivet for Sjælland, m.m., 1801–1803.
———. "Sageliste ved 4de Protocol." Copenhagen: Landsarkivet, 1801–1806.
———. "Sage-Liste ved Politi Retten, 2en Protocol." Copenhagen: Landsarkivet for Sjælland, m.m., 1801–1803.

Danish National Archives [Rigsarkivet], Copenhagen, Denmark

"Arrangements- og Liquidations-Commissionen i Handelshuset Blacks Enke & Co. [Erichsen Bankruptcy Papers]." *Eksekutorboer, 1790–1919*. Copenhagen: Rigsarkivet, 1833.

Balle, Nicolai Edinger. "Efterretninger om Kirke-, Fattige-, og Friskoler i København, insendt i Henhold til Danske Kancellis Cirkulære 10. juli 1790 [corrected to 1791]." Danske Kancelli, Kommission angaaende det almindelige Skolevæsen. 5a. Diverse. Copenhagen: Rigsarkivet, 1791.

Berling, Johan Carl Ernst. "Koncepter til Breve, m.m." Copenhagen: Rigsarkivet, 1867–1870.

———. "Materiale vedr. Bladet og Trykkeriet." Copenhagen: Rigsarkivet, 1748–1869.

Dansk Kancelli. Kommission ang. det almindelige Skolevæsen. 5a. "Diverse." Copenhagen: Rigsarkivet, 1790–91.

Københavns Skiftekommission, Hof- og Stadsretten. "Anette Linde's Probate." Forseglings Protokol, 199–203. Copenhagen: Rigsarkivet, 1814–1815.

———. "[Henrich Bonfils' Bankruptcy Papers, 1788]." Forseglings Protokol, 241–244. Copenhagen: Risgarkivet, 1780–1785.

———. "[Henrich Bonfils' Probate Records]." Forseglings Protokol, 72–77. Copenhagen: Rigsarkivet, 1771–1797.

———. "Samfrænde Brev, C.S. Black." Bevillinger og Samfrændeskiftebreve. Copenhagen: Rigsarkivet, 1783.

———. "Samfrænde Brev, Georg Christopher Berling." Bevillinger og Samfrændeskiftebreve. Copenhagen: Rigsarkivet, 1778.

———. "Samfrænde Brev Johanne Erichsen." Bevillinger og Samfrændeskiftebreve. Copenhagen: Rigsarkivet, 1800.

———. "Samfrænde Brev, P. Bonfils." Bevillinger og Samfrændeskiftebrev. Copenhagen: Rigsarkivet, 1788.

———. "Samfrænde Brev, Philibert Bonfils." Bevillinger og Samfrændeskiftebreve. Copenhagen: Rigsarkivet, 1771–1775.

Danish Business Archives [Erhvervsarkivet], Århus, Denmark [now in Viborg, Denmark]

Grosserer Societetet. "Alfabetisk Register til Forhandlingsprotokol." Århus, Denmark: Erhvervsarkivet, 1774–90.

———. "Forhandlingsprotokol." Århus, Denmark: Erhvervsarkivet, 1759–74, 1774–90, 1801.

———. "Journalsager." Århus, Denmark: Erhvervsarkivet, 1781–90, 1792–94, 1795–97, 1798–1800 and 1801–1804.

———. "Kopibog." Århus, Denmark: Erhvervsarkivet, 1787.

Danish Royal Library [Det kongelige Bibliotek], Copenhagen, Denmark

[Glasing, J.E.], ed. *Lejlighedsdigte fra den Berlingske Familie.* 2 vols. Copenhagen: unpublished, 1750–1808.

Published

"XIII. Forordning, hvorved den de Militaire her i Staden ... Fridhed at handle," Johan Jørgen Høpffner, ed. *Kong Christian den Siettes allernaadigste Forordninger og aabne Breve for Aar 1742.* Copenhagen: Hans kongel. Majest. og Universitets Bogtrykkerie, 1742.

Bech, Jens. *Forsøg til en moralsk Afhandling om Tarveligheds Indflydelse i et Folks Tilstand, Virksomhed og Sæder.* Copenhagen: Gyldendal, 1772.

Callisen, Henrich. *Physisk Medizinske Betragtninger over Kiöbenhavn.* 2 vols. Copenhagen: Frederik Brummers Forlag, 1807.

De til Forsendelse med Posten allene privilegerede Kiøbenhavnske Tidender. Copenhagen: Brødrene Berling, 1778, 1784, 1791, 1801.

Herr Ezechiel Gallatin's Franske Prædiken om Overdaadighed, translated [by Frederik Lütken]. Copenhagen: Nicolaus Møller, 1778.

Hammeleff, H. M. *Om den overdrevne Luxus i Hovedstaden og de bedste Midler til at hemme den.* Copenhagen: Bogbinder Brænnings Forlag, 1818.

Hauberg, [Ernst Christian], ed. *Kiøbenhavns kongelige Adresse-Contoirs Efterretninger.* Copenhagen: Morthorskee Enke & Comp. (?), 1801–.

Hertzberg, M. *Om Staters sande Rigdom, Handelens og Magrens Ligevegt.* Translated [from French]. Copenhagen: August Friderich Stein, 1786.

Holberg, Ludvig, "Epistola XCI." in F.J. Billeskov-Jansen, ed., *Ludvig Holberg: Værker i tolv bind: Digteren-Historikeren-Juristen.* Copenhagen: Rosenkilde & Bagge, 1969–71.

Kiøbenhavns kongelig allernaadigst privilergerede Adresse-Contoirs Efterretninger. Copenhagen: Simmelkiærs Enke, 1791.

En kort Samtale, hvorudt viises at Overdaadighed fornemmelig er Aarsag til endeel Borgeres ubillige og alt for store Klagemaal over svære Skatter og Bryder. Copenhagen: J.R. Thiele, 1772.

Lange, H., ed. *Vejviser, eller Anviisning til Kjøbenhavns, Christianshavns, samt Forstædernes Beboere.* Copenhagen: Boghandler L. Beeken, 1809.

Maanedskriftet Kiøbenhavns Skilderie. 3 vols. Copenhagen: Christ. Friderik Holm, 1787–1790.

Magazin for patriotiske Skribentere, hvori politiske, moralske og historiske Materier uden Bekostning indføres begynt med Skrive-Frieheden, vol. 1. Copenhagen: Adresse-Contoiret, 1771.

Meinert, Nicolai Jonathan. "Københavnerliv ombring 1800—Grosserer Nicolai Jonathan Meinerts erindringer ved redaktionen." *Historiske Meddelelser om København* (1970): 37–170.

[Moltke, Greve Frd. Ludvig]. *Breve om Overdaadighed og den skadelige Fölger i en Stat.* Copenhagen: Ludolph Henrich Lillie, [1758].

Nathan-David, [Chr. Georg]. "Hvorvidt har den indenlandske Handel i vidtudstrakte Statsterritorier fortrin for den udenlandske Handel." *Statsoeconomisk Archiv* 1 (1826): 173–211.

Nathanson, M.L. *Danmarks Handel, Skibsfart, Penge- og Finantsvæsen.* 3 vols. Copenhagen: C.A. Reitzel, 1832–34.

Nielsen, August, ed. *Samling af Bestemmelser vedrørende Københavns Kommune 1607–1839.* Copenhagen: J.H. Schultz, 1919.

Oehlenschläger, Adam. *Oehlenschlägers Erindringer.* 4 vols. Copenhagen: Andr. Fred. Høsts Forlag, 1850.

Petersen, Henrich. *Tanker til mine Medborgeres Eftertanke om Tarveligheds Indflydelse paa en Stat og dens Lyksalighed.* Odense: Iversen, 1783.

Proft, Enke, ed. *Vejviser eller Anviisning til Kjøbenhavns, Christianshavns og Forstædernes Beboere.* Copenhagen: C. Græbe, 1814, 1815.

Roth, T[yge]. *Tanker, i Anledning af den Preussiske Staats- og Cabinets-Ministers, Herren af Hertzbergs Tale, holden den 26de Januar. 1786, Hans Konges Fødselsdag.* Copenhagen: August Friderich Stein, Gyldendals Forlag, 1786.

Schou, Jacob Henric, ed. *Chronologisk Register over de kongelige Forordninger og aabne Breve*, vol. VIII. Copenhagen: L.C. Simmelkiær, 1784.

Seidelin, K.H., ed. *Politivennen*. Copenhagen, 1798 and 1801.

Sibbern, M. *Kiøbenhavnsbladet eller Borgeren og Politiet.* Copenhagen: C.F. Holm Enke, 1799–1807.

"Skilderie af vore Tider." *Et original Ugeblad*, 240. Copenhagen, 1790–91.

Smith, Adam. *Undersøgelse om National-Velstands Natur og Aarsag*, translated by F. Dræbye. 2 vols. Copenhagen: Gyldendals Forlag, 1779–1780.

Sommerfeldt, Christian. "Tanker om Overdaadighed og dens Virkninger," 1772.

Thiesen, Ludwig, ed. *Veiviser eller Anviisning til Kjøbenhavns og Forstædernes Beboer.* Copenhagen: Christopher Græbe, 1822.

"Tilskueren i Kiøbenhavn." *Et original Blad.* Copenhagen: Johan Friderich Morthorst, 1787–1788.

Tor-Stensen. *Tor-Stensens præliminaire Udkast til Overdaadigheds muelige Indskrænkning.* Copenhagen: Nicolaus Møller, 1780.

Wollstonecraft, Mary. *Letters Written During a Short Residence in Sweden, Norway, and Denmark.* London: J. Johnson, 1796.

Secondary Sources

in Danish

Bech, Svend Cedergreen. *Københavns historie gennem 800 år.* Copenhagen: P. Haase & Søns Forlag, 1967.

———. *Oplysning og Tolerance, 1721–1784. Danmarks Historie*, edited by John Danstrup and Hal Koch, vol. 9. Copenhagen: Politikens Forlag, 1965.

———. *Storhandelens By, 1728–1830. Københavns Historie*, edited by

Erik Kjersgaard, Svend Cedergreen Bech, and Jan Danielsen, vol. 3, 1728–1830, Copenhagen: Gyldendal, 1981.

Behrend, C. "Om nogle Skuespillerinder fra 18. og Beg. af 19. Aarhundrede." *Historiske Meddelelser om København*, 2nd series, vol. 3 (1927–28): 281–296.

———. "Om Nogle Skuespillerinder fra 18. og Beg. af 19. Aarhundrede." *Historiske Meddelelser om København*, 2nd series, vol. 4 (1929–30): 110–18, 381–87.

Bindslev, Alfred, ed. *København By og Erhverv gennem 500 Aar.* 2 vols. Copenhagen: Forlaget Novografia, 1948.

Blünikow, Bent. "Ernst Henrich Berling og hans fingeraftryk." *Berlingske Tidende*, March 21, 2008.

Bregnsbo, Michael. *Folk skriver til Kongen—Supplikkerne og deres funktion i den Danske-Norske enevælde i 1700-tallet.* Copenhagen: Selskabet for Udgivelse af Kilder til Dansk Historie, 1997.

Brodthagen, K.T. "Børshandel og Bankvæsen." *København By og Erhverv gennem 500 Aar*, edited by Alfred Bindslev. Copenhagen: Forlaget Novografia, 1948.

Bruun, Carl. *Kjøbenhavn. En illustreret Skildring af dets Historie, Mindesmærker og Institutioner*, vol. 3. Copenhagen: Det nordiske Forlag, 1901.

Christensen, John, and Henrik Stevnsborg. "Hos 'Madame Muurskee' i Dybensgade Nr. 200—Dagligliv i et Bordel i 1770'ernes København." *Historiske Meddelelser om København* (1982): 38–68.

———. "Politi og Prostituerede i 1790'ernes København." *Historiske Meddelelser om København* (1977): 164–83.

Clausen, Jul. *Berlingske Tidende 1749–1899.* Copenhagen: Berlingske Tidendes Officin ved P. Schmidt, 1899.

Dahl, Flemming. *Københvans Bystyre gennem 300 Aar*, vol. I: 1648–1858. Copenhagen: Ejnar Munksgaards Forlag, 1943.

Davidsen, J. *Fra det gamle Kongens København.* Copenhagen: Gyldendal, 1910.

Dübeck, Inger. *Købekoner og konkurrence.* Copenhagen: Juristforbundets Forlag, 1978.

———. *Kvinder, familie og formue—studier i Dansk og Europæisk retshistorie.* Copenhagen: Museum Tusculanums Forlag, 2003.

———, and Vagn Dybdahl. *Håndværkets kulturhistorie: Håndværket og statsmagten, perioden 1700–1862*, vol. 3. Copenhagen: Håndværksrådets Forlag, i kommission hos Schultz Forlag, 1983.

Edelberg, Peter. "De ældste led af slægten Fenger." Unpublished manuscript, Copenhagen (?), 2006. Author's private collection.

Ekberger, Maria. "Andreas Bodenhoff: Leverandør til søetaten i det 18. århundrede." *Maritim Kontakt* 13 (1989): 34–49.

Fabritius, Albert. *Grosserer-Societetets Præsidium, Komite og Repræsentantskab m.v. 1742–1942*. Copenhagen: [1942 ?].

Feldbæk, Ole. *Danmarks økonomiske historie, 1500–1840*. Herning, Denmark: Systime, 1993.

———. "Vækst og Reformer—Dansk forvaltning 1720–1814." *Dansk Forvaltningshistorie I—stat, forvaltning og samfund, fra middelalderen til 1901*, edited by Leon Jespersen and E. Ladewig Petersen. Copenhagen: Jurist- og økonomforbundets forlag, 2000.

Foltmar, Kaj. "Frøken Frederica Louise Ernst, fabrikant og negotiant i Københavns florissante handelstid." *Historiske Meddelelser om København* (1966): 81–140.

Hansen, Svend Aage. *Økonomiske vækst i Danmark*, vol. 1. Copenhagen: Universitetsforlag i København, G.E.C. Gads Forlag, 1972.

Hartby, Inger, Kirsten Jexlev, Kirsten Rykind-Eriksen, and Anne Røssell. "Handelsmadammer i 1700-Tallet." *Siden Saxo* 4, no. 3 (1987 1987): 29–36.

———. "Kvindeliv inden for håndværk og handel i 1700-tallet." *Livsstykker*, edited by Lone Rahbek Christensen. Ringe, Denmark: Kulturbøger, 1989.

———. *Madammer og Jomfruer—1700-tals kvinder i håndværk og handel*. Copenhagen: Nationalmuseet, 1986.

Hartmann, Sys, and Godfred Hartmann. *Kgs. Nytorv, Rosenborg og Nyboder. København før og nu—og aldrig*, edited by Bo Bramsen, vol. 5. Copenhagen: Palle Fogtdal, 1988.

Henningsen, Peter, and Ulrik Langen. *Hundemordet i Vimmelskaftet—og andre fortællinger fra 1700-tallets København*. Copenhagen: Jyllands-Postens Forlag, 2010.

Historiske Meddelelser om København. Copenhagen: Selskabet for Københavns Historie, 1907–2006.

Hyldtoft, Ole. *Danmarks økonomiske historie 1840–1910*. Århus: Systime, 1999.

———. *Mad, drikke og tobak 1800–35*. Copenhagen: Museum Tusculanums Forlag, 2012.

Ilsøe, Grethe, Karen Hjorth, and Birgitte Possing, eds. *Søg—og I skal finde—Udstilling*. Copenhagen: ARKI.Varia, 1991.

Ilsøe, Harald. *Bogtrykkerne i København og deres virksomhed ca. 1600–1810*. Copenhagen: Det Kongelige Bibliotek & Museum Tusculanums Forlag, 1992.

Jansen, Chr. R., ed. *Grosserer-Societetets Arkiv—En registratur*. Århus, Denmark: Erhvervsarkivet & Universitetsforlaget i Århus, 1983.

Jessen, Franz v. *To Hundrede Aar Berlingske Tidende 1749 3. Januar 1949*. Copenhagen: Det Berlingske Bogtrykkeri, 1949.

Jørgensen, Harald. "Carl Hieronimus Gustmeyer." *Dansk Biografisk Leksikon*, edited by Sv. Cedergreen Bech, p. 396. Copenhagen: Gyldendal, 1980.

———. "Erich Erichsen." *Dansk Biografisk Leksikon*, edited by Sv. Cedergreen Bech, p. 205. Copenhagen: Gyldendal, 1980.

Klæstrup, P. *Det Forsvundne Kjøbenhavn—Minder fra "De gode gamle Dage."* 3 vols. Copenhagen: C.A. Reitzel and Otto B. Wroblewsky, 1877.

Klug-Andersen, C. "Torvehandelen." *København By og Erhverv gennem 500 Aar*, edited by Alfred Bindslev. Copenhagen: Forlaget Novografia, 1948.

Kühle, Sejer. "Jyske Hosekræmmere i København i det 18. Aahundrede." *Historiske Meddelelser om København*, 3rd series, vol. 2 (1939): 163–83.

Lange, Nanna. *Den Bodenhoffske Slægtebog*. Copenhagen: A. Rosenbergs Bogtrykkeri, 1914.

Larsen, Jørgen. "Berlingske flytter til Pilestræde." *Berlingske Tidende*, August 13, 2008.

Larsen, Jytte, et al., ed. *Dansk Kvindebiografisk Leksikon*. 4 vols. Copenhagen: Rosinante, 2000.

Liisberg, Bering, and Jul. Schovelin. *De Danske Byerhverv i Tekst og Billeder*. Copenhagen: Lehmann & Stage, 1904.

Linde, Helle. "At skilles fra bord og seng—separationer i København 1813 og 1843." *Historiske Meddelelser om København* (1993): 165–84.

———. "Endnu ikke gift—Enker i København i første halvdel af 1800-tallet." *Handlingens Kvinder*, edited by Anette Warring and

Karen Hjorthe. Roskilde, Denmark: Roskilde Universitetsforlag, 2001.

———. "Jyder, Jøder og manufakturhandlere—Hosekræmmere i København 1700–1856." *Historiske Meddelelser om København* (2002): 50–75.

———. "Modehandel og kasketsalg—kvinder som selvstændige næringsdrivende i København 1845." *Søg—og I skal finde*, edited by Grethe Ilsøe, Karen Hjorth, and Birgitte Possing. Copenhagen: ARKI.Varia, 1991: 79–87.

———. "Skilsmisser i 1800-tallets København." *Københavns kronik* 50 (October 1990): 4–5.

Linvald, Steffen. *I portenes skygge*. Copenhagen: Stig Vendelkærs Forlag, 1965.

Lorenzen, Vilh., ed. *Grosserer-Societetet 1742–1942*. Copenhagen: Gyldendal, 1942.

Madsen, Hans Helge. *Interiørdekorationer i Erichsens Palæ—Fra arkitekten J.J. Ramé's virke i København*. Copenhagen: Aktieselskabet Kjøbenhavns Handelsbank, 1968.

Møller, Jan. *Borger i Holbergs København*. Copenhagen: Sesam, 1982.

———. *Borger i voldenes København*. Copenhagen: Sesam, 1978.

Norrie, Gordon. *Det danske Jordemodervæsens Historie. Danmarks Jordemødre*, edited by W. Nellemose, vol. 1. Copenhagen: Dansk Medicinsk-historisk Selskab, 1935.

Nystrøm, Eiler. "Henning Frederik Bargum." *Dansk Biografisk Leksikon*, edited by Sv. Cedergreen Bech. Copenhagen: Gyldendal, 1980.

Pedersen, Mikkel Venborg. *Luksus—Forbrug og kolonier i Danmark i det 18. århundrede*. Copenhagen: Museum Tusculanums Forlag, 2013.

Rasmussen, Edit. "Tømrerstrejken i København 1794 og dens omfang." *Historiske Meddelelser om København* (1984): 69–85.

Sandau, T.M. "Sankt Annæs Plads 11." Indenforvoldene.dk.

Schepelern, H.D. "Handel og Søfart i det 18. Aarhundrede." *København By og Erhverv gennem 500 Aar*, edited by Alfred Bindslev. Copenhagen: Forlaget Novografia, 1948.

Schovelin, Jul. *Fra den Danske Handels Empire—Forhold og Personer i det 18. Aarhundredes sidste Halvdel*. 2 vols. Copenhagen: Det nordiske Forlag, 1899–1900.

Søgaard, Helge. "Lidet om Københavns Brændevinsbrænderlav i det

18. Aarhundrede." *Historiske Meddelelser om København*, 3rd series, vol. 4 (1940–41): 473–503.
Thomsen, Niels, and Jette Søllinge. *De danske aviser 1634–1989*, vol. 1. Odense: Odense Universitetsforlag, 1987.
Vibæk, Jens. *Reform og Fallit, 1784–1830. Danmarks Historie*, edited by John Danstrup and Hal Koch, vol. 10. Copenhagen: Politikens Forlag, 1964.
Vogel-Jørgensen, T. *Berlingske Tidende gennem to Hundrede Aar, 1749–1949*. 3 vols. Copenhagen: Det Berlingske Bogtrykkeri, 1949.
———. "Da Flyttelæssene arriverede i Pilestræde 3. April 1765." Copenhagen: Det Berlingske Bogtrykkeri, 1930.
Wamberg, Bodil. *Grevinden—Et portræt af Grevinde Danner*. Copenhagen: Bogklubben, 2005.
Werner, Johannes. *Christian Wilhelm Duntzfelt. En Dansk Storkøbmand fra den glimrende Handelsperiode, Skildringer*. Copenhagen: Gyldendal, 1927.
West, Fritz Jürgensen, and William Norvin. *Berlingske Tidende—Udsigt over de Berlingske Avisers og den Danske Bogtrykkerslægt Berlings Historie*, vol. 1: 1749–1838. Copenhagen: Det Berlingske Bogtrykkeri, 1924.
Willerslev, Richard. "Boligforhold og befolkningstruktur i København o. 1800." *Historiske Meddelelser om København* (1983): 55 –80.
———. "Boligforholdene i København o. 1800." *Historiske Meddelelser om København* (1984): 86–121.
———, and P.P. Sveistrup. *Den Danske Sukkerhandels og Sukkerproduktions Historie*. Copenhagen: Institut for Historie og Samfundsøkonomi, Gyldendalske Boghandel, 1945.
Wolf, Edward C.J., and Gunnar Gregersen. "Haandværk." *København By og Erhverv gennem 500 Aar*, edited by Alfred Bindslev. Copenhagen: Forlaget Novografia, 1948.

in English

Barker, Hannah. *The Business of Women: Female Enterprise and Urban Development in Northern England, 1760–1830*. Oxford: Oxford University Press, 2006.
———, ed. "Women, Work and the Industrial Revolution: Female

Involvement in the English Printing Trades, c. 1700–1840." *Gender in Eighteenth-Century England*. London: Longman, 1997.

———, and Elaine Chalus, eds. *Gender in Eighteenth-Century England: Roles, Representations and Responsibilities*. London: Longman, 1997.

Berg, Maxine, and Helen Clifford, eds. *Consumers and Luxury: Consumer Culture in Europe, 1650–1850*. Manchester and New York: Manchester University Press, 1999.

Clark, Alice. *Working Life of Women in the Seventeenth Century*. London: George Routledge and Sons, Ltd., 1919.

Davis, Natalie Zemon. *Fiction in the Archives: Pardon Tales and the Tellers in Sixteenth-Century France*. Stanford, CA: Stanford University Press, 1987.

———. "Women in the Crafts in Sixteenth-Century Lyon." *Feminist Studies* 8, no. 1 (spring 1982): 46–80.

———. "'Women's History' in Transition: The European Case." *Feminist Studies* 3, no. 3/4 (spring–summer 1976): 83–103.

Dübeck, Inger. "Property and Authority in Danish Marital Law." *The Marital Economy in Scandinavia and Britain, 1400–1900*, edited by Maria Ågren and Amy Louise Erickson. Aldershot, UK: Ashgate, 2005.

Earle, Peter. "The Female Labour Market in the Late Seventeenth and Early Eighteenth Centuries." *The Economic History Review* 42, no. 3 (August 1989): 328–53.

Erickson, Amy Louise. "Married Women's Occupations in Eighteenth Century London." *Continuity and Change* 23, no. 2 (August 2008): 267–307.

George, M. Dorothy. *London Life in the Eighteenth Century*. London: Penguin, 1966.

Gold, Carol. "Copenhagen School Keepers 1790–1820." Database available in Københavns Stadsarkiv. Copenhagen, 1996. starbas.dk/pdf/schoolkeepers_database.pdf

———. *Danish Cookbooks: Domesticity and National Identity*. Seattle and Copenhagen: University of Washington Press and Museum Tusculanum Press, 2007.

———. *Educating Middle Class Daughters: Private Girls Schools in Copenhagen, 1790–1820*. Copenhagen: Museum Tusculanum Press, 1996.

———. "On the Streets and in the Markets: Independent Copenhagen

Saleswomen." *Female Agency in the Urban Economy: Gender in European Towns, 1640–1830*, edited by Deborah Simonton and Anne Montenach. New York and London: Routledge, 2013.

———. "The Danish Reform Era, 1784–1800." Ph.D. dissertation, University of Wisconsin–Madison, 1975.

———. "Women in the Late Eighteenth-Century Copenhagen Luxury Trades." *Luxury and Gender in European Towns, 1700–1914*, edited by Deborah Simonton, Marjo Kaartinen, and Anne Montenach. New York and London: Routledge, 2015.

Goody, Jack. *The European Family: An Historico-Anthropological Essay*. Oxford: Blackwell, 2000.

Hafter, Daryl, ed. *European Women and Preindustrial Craft*. Bloomington and Indianapolis: Indiana University Press, 1995.

———. *Women at Work in Preindustrial France*. University Park: The Pennsylvania State University Press, 2007.

Hall, Catherine. "Strains in the 'Firm of Wife, Children and Friends'? Middle-Class Women and Employment in Early Nineteenth-Century England." *Women's Work and the Family Economy in Historical Perspective*, edited by Pat Hudson and W.R. Lee. Manchester: University of Manchester Press, 1990.

Hill, Bridget, ed. *Eighteenth Century Women: An Anthology*. London: Allen & Unwin, 1984.

Horrell, Sara, and Jane Humphries. "Old Questions, New Data, and Alternative Perspectives: Families' Living Standards in the Industrial Revolution." *Journal of Economic History* 52, no. 4 (December 1992): 849–80.

———. "Women's Labour Force Participation and the Transition to the Male-Breadwinner Family, 1790–1865." *The Economic History Review* 48, no. 1 (1995): 89–117.

Hudson, Pat, and W.R. Lee, eds. *Women's Work and the Family Economy in Historical Perspective*. Manchester: Manchester University Press, 1990.

Hufton, Olwen. *The Prospect before Her: A History of Women in Western Europe, 1500–1800*. New York: Alfred A. Knopf, 1996.

———. "Women and the Family Economy in Eighteenth Century France." *French Historical Studies* (March 1, 1975): 1–22.

———. "Women without Men: Widows and Spinsters in Britain and

France in the Eighteenth Century." *Journal of Family History* 9, no. 4 (Winter 1984): 355–76.

Hunt, Margaret R. *The Middling Sort: Commerce, Gender, and the Family in England, 1680–1780*. Berkeley: University of California Press, 1996.

———. *Women in Eighteenth-Century Europe*. Harlow, UK: Longman, 2010.

Munck, Thomas. *The Enlightenment: A Comparative Social History 1721–1794*. London: Arnold, 2000.

Phillips, Nicola. *Women in Business, 1700–1850*. Woodbridge, Suffolk, UK: The Boydell Press, 2006.

Prior, Mary. "Women and the Urban Economy: Oxford 1500–1800." *Women in English Society 1500–1800*, edited by Mary Prior. London and New York: Methuen, 1985.

Rabuzzi, Daniel A. "Fading Images, Fading Realities? Female Merchants in Scandinavia and the Baltic." *Social History/Histoire Sociale* 34, no. 68 (2001): 355–70.

Schivelbusch, Wolfgang. *Tastes of Paradise: A Social History of Spices, Stimulants, and Intoxicants*. New York: Vintage, 1992.

Scott, Joan W., and Louise A. Tilly. *Women, Work, and Family*. New York: Holt, Rinehart and Winston, 1978.

Sharpe, Pamela. "Dealing with Love: The Ambiguous Independence of the Single Woman in Early Modern England." *Gender & History* 11, no. 2 (July 1999): 209–32.

Simonton, Deborah. "Claiming Their Place in the Corporate Community: Women's Identity in Eighteenth-Century Towns." *The Invisible Woman: Aspects of Women's Work in Eighteenth-Century Britain*, edited by Isabelle Baudino, Jacques Carré, and Cécile Révauger. Aldershot, UK: Ashgate, 2005.

———. *A History of European Women's Work: 1700 to the Present*. London: Routledge, 1998.

———. "Negotiating the Economy of the Eighteenth-Century Town: Female Entrepreneurs Claim Their Place." Paper presented at the American Historical Association Annual Conference, San Diego, CA, January, 2010.

———, and Anne Montenach, eds. *Female Agency in the Urban Economy: Gender in European Towns, 1640–1830*. London: Routledge, 2013.

———, Marjo Kaartinen, and Anne Montenach, eds. *Luxury and*

Gender in European Towns, 1799–1914. New York and London: Routledge, 2015.

Spang, Rebecca L. *The Invention of the Restaurant: Paris and Modern Gastronomic Culture*. Cambridge, MA, and London: Harvard University Press, 2000.

Tilly, Louise A., and Joan W. Scott. "Women's Work and the Family in Nineteenth-Century Europe." *The Economics of Women and Work*, edited by Alice H. Amsden. New York: St. Martin's Press, 1980.

Ulrich, Laurel Thatcher. *Well-Behaved Women Seldom Make History*. New York: Vintage Books, 2007.

Vainio-Korhonen, Kirsi. "Handicrafts as Professions and Sources of Income in Late Eighteenth and Early Nineteenth Century Turku (Åbo): A Gender Viewpoint to Economic History." *Scandinavian Economic History Review* XLVIII, no. 1 (2000): 40–63.

van den Heuvel, Danielle, and Elise van Nederveen Meerkerk, eds. "Partners in Business? Spousal Cooperation in Trades in Early Modern England and the Dutch Republic." Special issue, *Continuity and Change* 23, no. 2 (August 2008): 209–16.

Vickery, Amanda. *Behind Closed Doors: At Home in Georgian England*. New Haven, CT, and London: Yale University Press, 2009.

———. "Golden Age to Separate Spheres? A Review of the Categories and Chronology of English Women's History." *The Historical Journal* 36, no. 2 (June 1993): 383–414.

———. *The Gentleman's Daughter: Women's Lives in Georgian England*. New Haven, CT: Yale University Press, 1998.

Watkins, Priscilla G. "History of Estate Whim Museum." St. Croix Landmarks Society, http://www.stcroixlandmarks.com/history/estate-whim.

Index